YORK NOTES

POWER AND CONFLICT

AQA POETRY ANTHOLOGY

WORKBOOK BY BETH KEMP

Pearson

YORK PRESS

The right of Beth Kemp to be identified as the Author of this Work
has been asserted by her in accordance with the Copyright,
Designs and Patents Act 1988

YORK PRESS
322 Old Brompton Road, London SW5 9JH

PEARSON EDUCATION LIMITED
Edinburgh Gate, Harlow,
Essex CM20 2JE, United Kingdom
Associated companies, branches and representatives throughout the world

© Librairie du Liban *Publishers* 2018

First published 2018

10 9 8 7 6 5 4 3 2 1

ISBN 978-1-2922-3679-7

Phototypeset by Border Consultants Ltd
Printed in Slovakia

Text credits: 'Storm on the Island' from *Poems* 1965–1975 by Seamus Heaney. Copyright © 1980 by Seamus
Heaney. Reprinted by permission of Farrar, Straus and Giroux and Faber and Faber Ltd. 'Bayonet Charge' from
Collected Poems by Ted Hughes. Copyright © 2003 by The Estate of Ted Hughes. Reprinted by permission of
Farrar, Straus and Giroux and Faber and Faber Ltd. 'Remains' by Simon Armitage from *The Not Dead*, 2008,
published by Pomona, reproduced by kind permission of Pomona. 'War Photographer' from *Standing Female
Nude* by Carol Ann Duffy. Published by Anvil Press Poetry, 1985. Copyright © Carol Ann Duffy. Reproduced by
permission of the author c/o Rogers, Coleridge & White Ltd., 20 Powis Mews, London W11 1JN. 'Tissue' by Imtiaz
Dharker from *The terrorist at my table* (Bloodaxe Books, 2006) reprinted with permission of Bloodaxe Books on
behalf of the author. www.bloodaxebooks.com. 'The Emigrée' by Carol Rumens reproduced by permission of the
author. 'Checking Out Me History' copyright © 1996 by John Agard reproduced by kind permission of John Agard
c/o Caroline Sheldon Literary Agency Ltd.

Photo credits: cornfield/Shutterstock for page 8 / Nadalina/Shutterstock for page 10 / Tomas Pavelka/Shutterstock
for page 18 / PHILMACDPHOTOGRAPHY/iStock for page 20 / DavidTB/Shutterstock for page 24 / Mike
Pellinni/Shutterstock for page 26 / vithib/iStock for page 28 / Polly Chong/Shutterstock for page 35/ Keith
Tarrier/Shutterstock for page 36 top / antorti/iStock for page 36 bottom / georgeclerk/iStock for page 39 / ESB
Basic/Shutterstock for page 45 / Piers Buxton/Shutterstock for page 46 / DEA/A. DAGLI ORTI/Contributor/Getty for
page 53 / Johncairns/iStock for page 56 / Studio_Dagdagaz/iStock for page 58 / fsamora/iStock for page 64

CONTENTS

Contacts

PART FOUR:
FORM, STRUCTURE AND LANGUAGE

PART FIVE:
COMPARING POEMS

PART SIX:
PROGRESS BOOSTER

PART ONE: GETTING STARTED

Preparing for assessment

HOW WILL I BE ASSESSED ON MY WORK ON *POWER AND CONFLICT*?

When studying the cluster, your work will be examined through these three Assessment Objectives:

Assessment Objectives	Wording	Worth thinking about ...
AO1	Read, understand and respond to texts. Students should be able to: • maintain a critical style and develop an informed personal response • use textual references, including quotations, to support and illustrate interpretations.	• How well do I know what happens, what people say, do, etc. in each poem? • What do *I* think about the key ideas in the poems? • How can I support my viewpoint in a really convincing way? • What are the best quotations to use and when should I use them?
AO2	Analyse the language, form and structure used by a writer to create meanings and effects, using relevant subject terminology where appropriate.	• What specific things do the poets 'do'? What choices has each poet made? (Why this particular word, phrase or image here? Why does this change occur at this point?) • What effects do these choices create – optimism, pessimism, ambiguity?
AO3 *	Show understanding of the relationships between texts and the contexts in which they were written.	• What can I learn about society from the poems? (What do they tell me about stereotypes and prejudice, for example?) • What was/is society like for the poets? Can I see this reflected in their poems?

* **AO3** is only assessed in relation to the cluster, and not in relation to the 'Unseen' part of the exam.

In other parts of your English Literature GCSE a fourth Assessment Objective, **AO4**, which is related to spelling, punctuation and grammar, is also assessed. While you will not gain any marks for AO4 in your poetry examination, it is still important to ensure that you write accurately and clearly, in order to get your points across to the examiner in the best possible way.

Look out for the Assessment Objective labels throughout your York Notes Workbook – these will help to focus your study and revision!

The text used in this Workbook is *Past and Present: Poetry Anthology* (AQA, 2015).

How to use your York Notes Workbook

There are lots of ways your Workbook can support your study and revision of the *Power and Conflict* poetry cluster. There is no 'right' way – choose the one that suits your learning style best.

1) Alongside the York Notes Study Guide and the text	2) As a 'stand-alone' revision programme	3) As a form of mock-exam
Do you have the York Notes Study Guide for *Power and Conflict*? The contents of your Workbook are designed to match the sections in the Study Guide, so with the poems to hand you could: • read the relevant section(s) of the Study Guide and the poems referred to; • complete the tasks in the same section in your Workbook.	Think you know *Power and Conflict* well? Why not work through the Workbook systematically, either as you finish reading the poems, or as you study or revise certain aspects in class or at home? You could make a revision diary and allocate particular sections of the Workbook to a day or week.	Prefer to do all your revision in one go? You could put aside a day or two and work through the Workbook, page by page. Once you have finished, check all your answers in one go! This will be quite a challenge, but it may be the approach you prefer.

HOW WILL THE WORKBOOK HELP YOU TEST AND CHECK YOUR KNOWLEDGE AND SKILLS?

Parts Two to **Five** offer a range of tasks and activities:

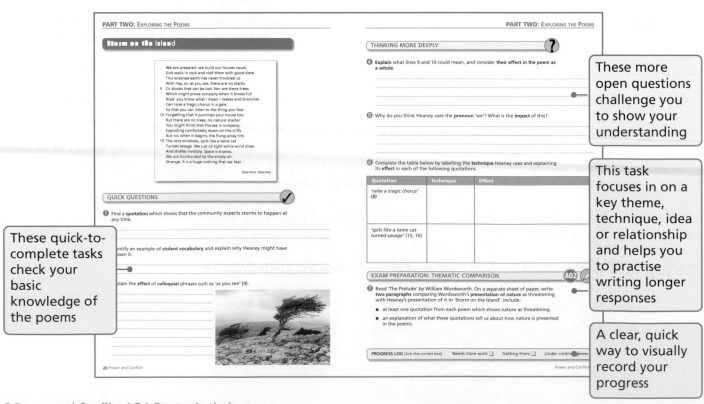

These quick-to-complete tasks check your basic knowledge of the poems

These more open questions challenge you to show your understanding

This task focuses in on a key theme, technique, idea or relationship and helps you to practise writing longer responses

A clear, quick way to visually record your progress

Each Part ends with a **Practice task** to extend your revision:

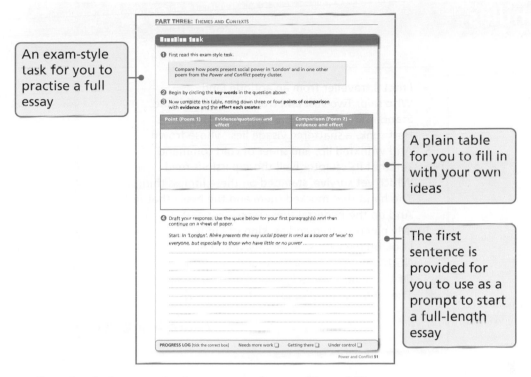

An exam-style task for you to practise a full essay

A plain table for you to fill in with your own ideas

The first sentence is provided for you to use as a prompt to start a full-length essay

Part Six: Progress Booster helps you test your own key writing skills:

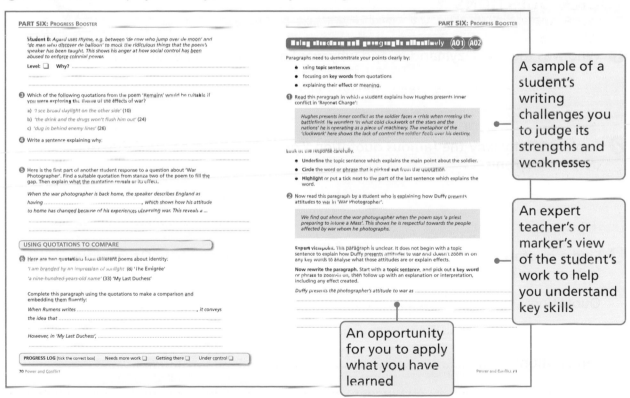

A sample of a student's writing challenges you to judge its strengths and weaknesses

An expert teacher's or marker's view of the student's work to help you understand key skills

An opportunity for you to apply what you have learned

Don't forget – these are just some examples of the Workbook contents. Inside there is much, much more to help you revise. For example:

- top tips on approaching tricky questions
- help with comparing poems
- advice and tasks on writing about context
- a full answer key so you can check your answers
- a full-length sample answer for you to annotate and grade.

PART TWO: EXPLORING THE POEMS

Ozymandias

I met a traveller from an antique land
Who said: Two vast and trunkless legs of stone
Stand in the desert. Near them on the sand,
Half sunk, a shattered visage lies, whose frown
5   And wrinkled lip, and sneer of cold command
Tell that its sculptor well those passions read
Which yet survive, stamped on these lifeless things,
The hand that mocked them and the heart that fed;
And on the pedestal these words appear:
10   'My name is Ozymandias, king of kings:
Look on my works, ye Mighty, and despair!'
Nothing beside remains. Round the decay
Of that colossal wreck, boundless and bare,
The lone and level sands stretch far away.

Percy Bysshe Shelley

QUICK QUESTIONS

1 Who was the real Ozymandias and why was Shelley writing about him?

....

....

2 **Explain** briefly why the famous quotation *'Look on my works, ye Mighty, and despair!'* is **ironic**.

....

....

3 Find a **quotation** from near the end of the poem that shows how Ozymandias lacks power now and **explain** what it implies.

Quotation: ....

....

Explanation: ....

....

THINKING MORE DEEPLY

4 Why do you think Shelley chooses to begin with *'I met a traveller'* (1)? What is the **effect** of **framing the narrative** of the poem like this?

....

....

....

5 How does Shelley build up an image of Ozymandias's arrogance? Complete the first example in the table below. Then add a second example showing a different technique.

Quotation	Technique	Effect
'sneer of cold command' (5)		

6 How does Shelley use **form** or **structure** to support his depiction of Ozymandias's loss of power?

....

....

....

....

....

7 What is Shelley trying to show by stating *'Nothing beside remains'* (12) after the inscription from the statue?

....

....

....

....

....

EXAM PREPARATION: POWER PORTRAYAL

8 Read 'My Last Duchess' by Robert Browning. On a separate sheet of paper, write **two paragraphs** comparing Browning's **presentation of arrogance** with Shelley's in 'Ozymandias'. Include:

- at least one quotation from each poem which shows the arrogance of Ozymandias or the Duke

- an explanation of what these quotations tell us about how arrogance is portrayed in the poems.

PROGRESS LOG [tick the correct box]   Needs more work ☐   Getting there ☐   Under control ☐

London

> I wander through each chartered street,
> Near where the chartered Thames does flow,
> And mark in every face I meet
> Marks of weakness, marks of woe.
>
> 5 In every cry of every man,
> In every infant's cry of fear,
> In every voice, in every ban,
> The mind-forged manacles I hear:
>
> How the chimney-sweeper's cry
> 10 Every black'ning church appalls,
> And the hapless soldier's sigh
> Runs in blood down palace walls.
>
> But most through midnight streets I hear
> How the youthful harlot's curse
> 15 Blasts the new-born infant's tear,
> And blights with plagues the marriage hearse.
>
> *William Blake*

QUICK QUESTIONS

1 Which word does Blake repeat in the **second stanza** to show that all of London is being affected by the misery he witnesses?

....

2 Find a **quotation** which shows Blake's dissatisfaction with rich people taking control of the city. Briefly explain the **effect** of this line/phrase.

Quotation: ....

....

Effect: ....

....

3 How does the poem's **rhythm** help to convey Blake's message?

....

....

....

....

....

....

....

THINKING MORE DEEPLY

4 What is the **effect** of first-person narrative in this poem? How does a **personal perspective** create an impact on the reader?

....

....

....

5 **Why** does Blake describe the people's manacles as *'mind-forged'* (8)?

....

....

....

....

6 Choose an example of **violent imagery** from the second half of the poem and comment on its effect. Why do you think the poem becomes more violent in tone as it goes on?

....

....

....

....

....

....

7 Why does Blake select *'the chimney-sweeper'*, *'the soldier'* and *'the harlot'* to write about?

....

....

....

....

EXAM PREPARATION: VIEWPOINT   **A02**

8 How would you describe the way in which the speaker views the people of London in the poem? On a separate sheet of paper, write **two paragraphs** exploring:

● the language the speaker uses to describe the people as a group

● an example of a specific person or image in more detail.

PROGRESS LOG [tick the correct box]   Needs more work ☐   Getting there ☐   Under control ☐

Extract from, 'The Prelude'

One summer evening (led by her) I found
A little boat tied to a willow tree
Within a rocky cove, its usual home.
Straight I unloosed her chain, and stepping in
5 Pushed from the shore. It was an act of stealth
And troubled pleasure, nor without the voice
Of mountain-echoes did my boat move on;
Leaving behind her still, on either side,
Small circles glittering idly in the moon,
10 Until they melted all into one track
Of sparkling light. But now, like one who rows,
Proud of his skill, to reach a chosen point
With an unswerving line, I fixed my view
Upon the summit of a craggy ridge,
15 The horizon's utmost boundary; far above
Was nothing but the stars and the grey sky.
She was an elfin pinnace; lustily
I dipped my oars into the silent lake,
And, as I rose upon the stroke, my boat
20 Went heaving through the water like a swan;
When, from behind that craggy steep till then
The horizon's bound, a huge peak, black and huge,

As if with voluntary power instinct,
Upreared its head. I struck and struck again,
25 And growing still in stature the grim shape
Towered up between me and the stars, and still,
For so it seemed, with purpose of its own
And measured motion like a living thing,
Strode after me. With trembling oars I turned,
30 And through the silent water stole my way
Back to the covert of the willow tree;
There in her mooring-place I left my bark, –
And through the meadows homeward went, in grave
And serious mood; but after I had seen
35 That spectacle, for many days, my brain
Worked with a dim and undetermined sense
Of unknown modes of being; o'er my thoughts
There hung a darkness, call it solitude
Or blank desertion. No familiar shapes
40 Remained, no pleasant images of trees,
Of sea or sky, no colours of green fields;
But huge and mighty forms, that do not live
Like living men, moved slowly through the mind
By day, and were a trouble to my dreams.

William Wordsworth

QUICK QUESTIONS

❶ Briefly **explain** what the speaker does in this poem.

....

....

❷ Choose a **quotation** that shows the speaker's enjoyment of nature at the start and **explain** how it implies this.

Quotation: ....

....

Explanation: ....

....

❸ Explain why Wordsworth repeats the simple word *'huge'* (22) instead of choosing more impressive **vocabulary**. What does this tell us about the speaker at this point?

....

....

....

THINKING MORE DEEPLY

4 How does Wordsworth use **personification** to support his theme in this poem? Choose a **quotation** and explain its **effect** to support your ideas.

Quotation: ....

....

Effect: ....

....

5 How do you think the poem's **form** supports its **theme**? Give **evidence** for your ideas.

....

....

....

6 Complete the table below. Choose **two quotations** that emphasise the power of the imagination in different ways. Name the technique or use of language and explain how Wordsworth achieves this **effect** in these lines/phrases.

Quotation	Technique	Effect

EXAM PREPARATION: COMPARISON BETWEEN POEMS

7 Read 'Remains' by Simon Armitage. On a separate sheet of paper, write **two paragraphs** comparing Armitage's presentation of **inner conflict** with Wordsworth's in 'The Prelude'. Include:

● at least one quotation from each poem which shows inner conflict

● an explanation of what these quotations tell us about how inner conflict is presented in the poems.

PROGRESS LOG [tick the correct box]   Needs more work ☐   Getting there ☐   Under control ☐

My Last Duchess

Ferrara

That's my last Duchess painted on the wall,
Looking as if she were alive. I call
That piece a wonder, now: Frà Pandolf's hands
Worked busily a day, and there she stands.
5 Will't please you sit and look at her? I said
'Frà Pandolf' by design, for never read
Strangers like you that pictured countenance,
The depth and passion of its earnest glance,
But to myself they turned (since none puts by
10 The curtain I have drawn for you, but I)
And seemed as they would ask me, if they durst,
How such a glance came there; so, not the first
Are you to turn and ask thus. Sir, 'twas not
Her husband's presence only, called that spot
15 Of joy into the Duchess' cheek: perhaps
Frà Pandolf chanced to say 'Her mantle laps
Over my lady's wrist too much,' or 'Paint
Must never hope to reproduce the faint
Half-flush that dies along her throat': such stuff
20 Was courtesy, she thought, and cause enough
For calling up that spot of joy. She had
A heart – how shall I say? – too soon made glad,
Too easily impressed; she liked whate'er
She looked on, and her looks went everywhere.
25 Sir, 'twas all one! My favour at her breast,
The dropping of the daylight in the West,
The bough of cherries some officious fool
Broke in the orchard for her, the white mule
She rode with round the terrace – all and each

30 Would draw from her alike the approving speech,
Or blush, at least. She thanked men, – good! but thanked
Somehow – I know not how – as if she ranked
My gift of a nine-hundred-years-old name
With anybody's gift. Who'd stoop to blame
35 This sort of trifling? Even had you skill
In speech – (which I have not) – to make your will
Quite clear to such an one, and say, 'Just this
Or that in you disgusts me; here you miss,
Or there exceed the mark' – and if she let
40 Herself be lessoned so, nor plainly set
Her wits to yours, forsooth, and made excuse,
– E'en then would be some stooping; and I choose
Never to stoop. Oh sir, she smiled, no doubt,
Whene'er I passed her; but who passed without
45 Much the same smile? This grew; I gave commands;
Then all smiles stopped together. There she stands
As if alive. Will't please you rise? We'll meet
The company below, then. I repeat,
The Count your master's known munificence
50 Is ample warrant that no just pretence
Of mine for dowry will be disallowed;
Though his fair daughter's self, as I avowed
At starting, is my object. Nay, we'll go
Together down, sir. Notice Neptune, though,
55 Taming a sea-horse, thought a rarity,
Which Claus of Innsbruck cast in bronze for me!

Robert Browning

QUICK QUESTIONS

❶ This poem is in the form of a **dramatic monologue**. Explain what this means.

....

....

❷ Why does *'none ... but I'* (9, 10) reveal the Duchess's portrait? What does this **detail** reveal to the reader?

....

....

....

❸ What type of **rhyme** is used throughout the poem? What is the **effect** of this rhyme scheme?

Rhyme: ....

Effect: ....

....

THINKING MORE DEEPLY

4 How does Browning encourage the reader not to take the Duke's accusations against his 'last' wife seriously? Give **evidence** to support your ideas.

....

....

....

....

....

5 What does the quotation *'my gift of a nine-hundred-years-old name'* (33) contribute to the **theme** of power? How does Browning create the relevant **impact** with this phrase?

....

....

....

....

....

6 How does Browning show us the Duke's misogynistic attitude? Choose **two quotations** which use different **language techniques** to demonstrate this. Explain their **effect** on the reader.

Quotation	Technique	Effect

EXAM PREPARATION: FOCUSING ON FORM

7 Choose an aspect of the Duke's **character** and, on a separate sheet of paper, write **two paragraphs** explaining:

- how Browning has presented this aspect to the reader

- how Browning uses the **dramatic monologue** form effectively in developing the character.

PROGRESS LOG [tick the correct box]　　Needs more work ☐　　Getting there ☐　　Under control ☐

The Charge of the Light Brigade

1.
Half a league, half a league,
Half a league onward,
All in the valley of Death
    Rode the six hundred.
5 'Forward, the Light Brigade!
Charge for the guns!' he said:
Into the valley of Death
    Rode the six hundred.

2.
'Forward, the Light Brigade!'
10 Was there a man dismay'd?
Not tho' the soldier knew
    Some one had blunder'd:
Theirs not to make reply,
Theirs not to reason why,
15 Theirs but to do and die:
Into the valley of Death
    Rode the six hundred.

3.
Cannon to right of them,
Cannon to left of them,
20 Cannon in front of them
    Volley'd and thunder'd;
Storm'd at with shot and shell,
Boldly they rode and well,
Into the jaws of Death,
25 Into the mouth of Hell
    Rode the six hundred.

4.
Flash'd all their sabres bare,
Flash'd as they turn'd in air
Sabring the gunners there,
30 Charging an army, while
    All the world wonder'd:
Plunged in the battery-smoke
Right thro' the line they broke;
Cossack and Russian
35 Reel'd from the sabre-stroke
    Shatter'd and sunder'd.
Then they rode back, but not
    Not the six hundred.

5.
Cannon to right of them,
40 Cannon to left of them,
Cannon behind them
    Volley'd and thunder'd;
Storm'd at with shot and shell,
While horse and hero fell,
45 They that had fought so well
Came thro' the jaws of Death,
Back from the mouth of Hell,
All that was left of them,
    Left of six hundred.

6.
50 When can their glory fade?
    O the wild charge they made!
    All the world wonder'd.
Honour the charge they made!
Honour the Light Brigade,
55   Noble six hundred!

Alfred Tennyson

QUICK QUESTIONS

1 Which **conflict** does this poem relate to?

....

2 How is the **dactylic dimeter** used in this poem effectively?

....

....

3 How does the **structure** of the poem help Tennyson convey his message to his readers?

....

....

....

THINKING MORE DEEPLY

4 Complete the table below by identifying the **technique** Tennyson is using in each quotation, and explaining its **effect**.

Quotation	Technique	Effect
'Into the valley of Death' (17)		
'Theirs not to make reply, Theirs not to reason why, Theirs but to do and die' (13–15)		

5 What would be the **effect** on the listener/reader of the **repetition** of *'six hundred'*?

....

....

....

6 How does Tennyson use **verbs** in this poem to have an **impact** on the reader? Use **evidence** to support your answer.

....

....

....

....

EXAM PREPARATION: COMPARISON OF THEME (A02)

7 Read 'Exposure' by Wilfred Owen. On a separate sheet of paper, write **two paragraphs** comparing Owen's **presentation** of the experience of battle with Tennyson's in 'The Charge of the Light Brigade'. Include:

- at least one quotation from each poem which shows the experience of battle

- an explanation of what these quotations tell us about how the experience of battle is presented in the poems.

PROGRESS LOG [tick the correct box]   Needs more work ☐   Getting there ☐   Under control ☐

Exposure

Our brains ache, in the merciless iced east winds that
          knive us ...
Wearied we keep awake because the night is silent ...
Low, drooping flares confuse our memory of the
          salient ...
Worried by silence, sentries whisper, curious, nervous,
5   But nothing happens.

Watching, we hear the mad gusts tugging on the wire,
Like twitching agonies of men among its brambles.
Northward, incessantly, the flickering gunnery rumbles,
Far off, like a dull rumour of some other war.
10   What are we doing here?

The poignant misery of dawn begins to grow ...
We only know war lasts, rain soaks, and clouds sag stormy.
Dawn massing in the east her melancholy army
Attacks once more in ranks on shivering ranks of grey,
15   But nothing happens.

Sudden successive flights of bullets streak the silence.
Less deadly than the air that shudders black with snow,
With sidelong flowing flakes that flock, pause, and renew,
We watch them wandering up and down the wind's
          nonchalance,
20   But nothing happens.

Pale flakes with fingering stealth come feeling for our
          faces –
We cringe in holes, back on forgotten dreams, and stare,
          snow-dazed,
Deep into grassier ditches. So we drowse, sun-dozed,
Littered with blossoms trickling where the blackbird fusses.
25   – Is it that we are dying?

Slowly our ghosts drag home: glimpsing the sunk fires,
          glozed
With crusted dark-red jewels; crickets jingle there;
For hours the innocent mice rejoice: the house is theirs;
Shutters and doors, all closed: on us the doors are closed, –
30   We turn back to our dying.

Since we believe not otherwise can kind fires burn;
Now ever suns smile true on child, or field, or fruit.
For God's invincible spring our love is made afraid;
Therefore, not loath, we lie out here; therefore were born,
35   For love of God seems dying.

Tonight, His frost will fasten on this mud and us,
Shrivelling many hands. puckering foreheads crisp.
The burying-party, picks and shovels in shaking grasp,
Pause over half-known faces. All their eyes are ice,
40   But nothing happens.

Wilfred Owen

QUICK QUESTIONS

1 Why is *'But nothing happens'* repeated (6, 16, 21, 43)?

....

....

2 What is the **effect** of Owen's unusual **personification** of the dawn in line 14?

....

....

3 Choose a quotation that shows Owen using **sound** effectively and explain the technique's **impact** on the reader.

Quotation: ....

....

....

Impact: ....

....

....

THINKING MORE DEEPLY

4 What is significant in the opening phrase *'Our brains ache'* (1)? Comment on Owen's **language choices** here, using appropriate **terminology** and explaining the **effect**.

....

....

....

....

5 What kind of **rhyme** does Owen use and how does this relate to the poem's **themes**?

....

....

....

....

6 How is the **weather portrayed** as more of a threat to the soldiers than the battle itself? Provide **evidence** to support your ideas.

....

....

....

....

7 Why does Owen include the **stanza about home**? What is the likely **effect** of this?

....

....

....

....

EXAM PREPARATION: ANALYSIS OF ATTITUDE A02

8 How would you comment on Owen's **presentation** of the soldiers' **attitude to war** in the poem? On a separate sheet of paper, write two paragraphs exploring:

- how the actual war is described in the poem
- what the soldiers' immediate concerns are.

PROGRESS LOG [tick the correct box]   Needs more work ☐   Getting there ☐   Under control ☐

Storm on the Island

> We are prepared: we build our houses squat,
> Sink walls in rock and roof them with good slate.
> This wizened earth has never troubled us
> With hay, so, as you see, there are no stacks
> 5 Or stooks that can be lost. Nor are there trees
> Which might prove company when it blows full
> Blast: you know what I mean – leaves and branches
> Can raise a tragic chorus in a gale
> So that you can listen to the thing you fear
> 10 Forgetting that it pummels your house too.
> But there are no trees, no natural shelter.
> You might think that the sea is company,
> Exploding comfortably down on the cliffs
> But no: when it begins, the flung spray hits
> 15 The very windows, spits like a tame cat
> Turned savage. We just sit tight while wind dives
> And strafes invisibly. Space is a salvo,
> We are bombarded by the empty air.
> Strange, it is a huge nothing that we fear.
>
> *Seamus Heaney*

QUICK QUESTIONS ✔

❶ Find a **quotation** which shows that the community expects storms to happen at any time.

....

....

❷ Identify an example of **violent vocabulary** and explain why Heaney might have chosen it.

....

....

❸ Explain the **effect** of **colloquial** phrases such as *'as you see'* (4).

....

....

....

....

....

....

....

THINKING MORE DEEPLY

4 **Explain** what lines 9 and 10 could mean, and consider **their effect in the poem as a whole**.

....

....

....

....

5 Why do you think Heaney uses the **pronoun** 'we'? What is the **impact** of this?

....

....

....

6 Complete the table below by labelling the **technique** Heaney uses and explaining its **effect** in each of the following quotations.

Quotation	Technique	Effect
'raise a tragic chorus' (8)		
'spits like a tame cat turned savage' (15, 16)		

EXAM PREPARATION: THEMATIC COMPARISON

7 Read 'The Prelude' by William Wordsworth. On a separate sheet of paper, write **two paragraphs** comparing Wordsworth's **presentation of nature** as threatening with Heaney's presentation of it in 'Storm on the Island'. Include:

- at least one quotation from each poem which shows nature as threatening

- an explanation of what these quotations tell us about how nature is presented in the poems.

PROGRESS LOG [tick the correct box]   Needs more work ☐   Getting there ☐   Under control ☐

Bayonet Charge

Suddenly he awoke and was running – raw
In raw-seamed hot khaki, his sweat heavy,
Stumbling across a field of clods towards a green hedge
That dazzled with rifle fire, hearing
5 Bullets smacking the belly out of the air –
He lugged a rifle numb as a smashed arm;
The patriotic tear that had brimmed in his eye
Sweating like molten iron from the centre of his chest, –

In bewilderment then he almost stopped –
10 In what cold clockwork of the stars and the nations
Was he the hand pointing that second? He was running
Like a man who has jumped up in the dark and runs
Listening between his footfalls for the reason
Of his still running, and his foot hung like
15 Statuary in mid-stride. Then the shot-slashed furrows

Threw up a yellow hare that rolled like a flame
And crawled in a threshing circle, its mouth wide
Open silent, its eyes standing out.
He plunged past with his bayonet toward the green hedge,
20 King, honour, human dignity, etcetera
Dropped like luxuries in a yelling alarm
To get out of that blue crackling air
His terror's touchy dynamite.

Ted Hughes

QUICK QUESTIONS

❶ Find a quotation which shows that the soldier is experiencing a moment of confusion.

....

....

❷ What is the **effect** of repeating *'raw'* (1, 2)?

....

....

❸ Find an example of **physical imagery** in the **first stanza** and explain its **effect**.

Image: ....

....

Effect: ....

....

....

THINKING MORE DEEPLY

4 How does the 'clockwork' image (10, 11) add to the poem's **theme**? What do you think the reader is supposed to understand from these lines?

....
....
....
....

5 How does Hughes evoke the different senses in this poem? Comment on the **impact** of this **sensory imagery**, providing **evidence** for your ideas.

....
....
....
....
....

6 Why is the hare (16) a **turning point** in this poem? Support your ideas with **evidence**.

....
....
....
....

7 What is Hughes suggesting with the quotation *'King, honour, human dignity, etcetera'* (20) and how does he create his **desired impact** with this line?

....
....
....
....

EXAM PREPARATION: CONTRASTS WITHIN A POEM   **A02**

8 How does Hughes show a **contrast** between the ideals of patriotism and the harsh reality of battle in this poem? On a separate sheet of paper, write **two paragraphs** exploring:

- how patriotic ideals are presented
- how harsh reality is shown.

PROGRESS LOG [tick the correct box]   Needs more work ❑   Getting there ❑   Under control ❑

Remains

On another occasion, we get sent out
to tackle looters raiding a bank.
And one of them legs it up the road,
probably armed, possibly not.

5 Well myself and somebody else and somebody else
are all of the same mind,
so all three of us open fire.
Three of a kind all letting fly, and I swear

I see every round as it rips through his life –
10 I see broad daylight on the other side.
So we've hit this looter a dozen times
and he's there on the ground, sort of inside out,

pain itself, the image of agony.
One of my mates goes by
15 and tosses his guts back into his body.
Then he's carted off in the back of a lorry.

End of story, except not really.
His blood-shadow stays on the street, and out on patrol
I walk right over it week after week.
20 Then I'm home on leave. But I blink

and he bursts again through the doors of the bank.
Sleep, and he's probably armed, possibly not.
Dream, and he's torn apart by a dozen rounds.
And the drink and the drugs won't flush him out –

25 he's here in my head when I close my eyes,
dug in behind enemy lines,
not left for dead in some distant, sun-stunned,
   sand-smothered land
or six-feet-under in desert sand,

but near to the knuckle, here and now,
30 his bloody life in my bloody hands.

Simon Armitage

QUICK QUESTIONS

1 Explain briefly what happens in this poem.

....

....

....

2 Find an example of a **colloquial** phrase in the **first stanza** and explain its **effect**.

Colloquial phrase: ....

Effect: ....

....

3 What is the **effect** of the phrase *'blood-shadow'* (18)?

....

....

....

....

....

....

THINKING MORE DEEPLY

4 What **different meanings** does the **title** 'Remains' convey?

....

....

....

....

5 Why do you think Armitage uses such a **conversational tone** for this poem? How does this help create an **impact**? Give **evidence** to support your ideas.

....

....

....

....

....

6 Complete the table below with appropriate **terminology, quotations** and **explanations**.

Technique	Quotation	Effect
Idiom		
	'it rips through his life' (9)	

EXAM PREPARATION: ANALYSIS OF DETAIL

7 How would you **explain** the way in which Armitage shows us the **speaker's mental state** in this poem? On a separate sheet of paper, write **two paragraphs** exploring:

- how Armitage shows us the important moment
- how Armitage shows us his inability to forget.

Poppies

QUICK QUESTIONS

1 Who is the **speaker** in this poem?

....

....

2 Find an example of **imagery** relating to pain in the **first stanza**. What is its **impact**?

....

....

3 What **technique** does Weir use to imply crying, when she describes the song bird in line 24? What is the **effect** of describing it in this way?

Technique: ....

....

Effect:..

....

....

THINKING MORE DEEPLY

?

④ How does Weir use **references to time** in this poem to support her **themes**?

....

....

....

....

⑤ Complete the table below by identifying the **techniques** and explaining their **effects**:

Example	Technique	Effect
Lines 20, 21		
Lines 27, 28		
Lines 10, 11		

⑥ Explain how the poem's **form** helps to support its **themes**.

....

....

....

....

EXAM PREPARATION: COMPARISON OF VIEWPOINT

A02

⑦ Read 'Kamikaze' by Beatrice Garland. On a separate sheet of paper, write **two paragraphs** comparing Garland's use of **viewpoint** with Weir's in 'Poppies'. Include:

● at least one quotation from each poem which shows how viewpoint is used

● an explanation of what these quotations tell us about how viewpoint is used in the poems.

PROGRESS LOG [tick the correct box]   Needs more work ☐   Getting there ☐   Under control ☐

War Photographer

In his darkroom he is finally alone
with spools of suffering set out in ordered rows.
The only light is red and softly glows,
as though this were a church and he
5 a priest preparing to intone a Mass.
Belfast. Beirut. Phnom Penh. All flesh is grass.

He has a job to do. Solutions slop in trays
beneath his hands, which did not tremble then
though seem to now. Rural England. Home again
10 to ordinary pain which simple weather can dispel,
to fields which don't explode beneath the feet
of running children in a nightmare heat.

Something is happening. A stranger's features
faintly start to twist before his eyes,
15 a half-formed ghost. He remembers the cries
of this man's wife, how he sought approval
without words to do what someone must
and how the blood stained into foreign dust.

A hundred agonies in black-and-white
20 from which his editor will pick out five or six
for Sunday's supplement. The reader's eyeballs prick
with tears between the bath and pre-lunch beers.
From the aeroplane he stares impassively at where
he earns his living and they do not care.

Carol Ann Duffy

QUICK QUESTIONS

1 Where does the **allusion** *'All flesh is grass'* (6) come from and what does it mean?

....

....

2 Find a quotation in the **first stanza** that shows the photographer's respectful **attitude** towards his work and explain how Duffy reveals this.

Quotation: ....

....

....

....

How it reveals his respectful attitude: ....

....

....

....

THINKING MORE DEEPLY

3 How do you think the **use of voice** in this poem supports its central **message**?

....

....

....

....

....

4 How does Duffy **portray** the photographer's home? Support your ideas with **evidence**.

....

....

....

....

....

5 What is the **significance** of the following quotations? Label the **techniques** and explain their **effect**.

Quotation	Technique	Effect
'He has a job to do.' (7)		
'The reader's eyeballs prick with tears between the bath and pre-lunch beers.' (21, 22)		

EXAM PREPARATION: COMPARISON OF VIEWPOINT (A02)

6 How would you describe the way in which the war photographer views his **work** in the poem? On a separate sheet of paper, write **two paragraphs** exploring:

● how he approaches his work

● what he seems to think about his work.

PROGRESS LOG [tick the correct box]   Needs more work ☐   Getting there ☐   Under control ☐

Tissue

Paper that lets the light
shine through, this
is what could alter things.
Paper thinned by age or touching,

5 the kind you find in well-used books,
the back of the Koran, where a hand
has written in the names and histories,
who was born to whom,

the height and weight, who
10 died where and how, on which sepia date,
pages smoothed and stroked and turned
transparent with attention.

If buildings were paper, I might
feel their drift, see how easily
15 they fall away on a sigh, a shift
in the direction of the wind.

Maps too. The sun shines through
their borderlines, the marks
that rivers make, roads,
20 railtracks, mountainfolds,

Fine slips from grocery shops
that say how much was sold
and what was paid by credit card
might fly our lives like paper kites.

25 An architect could use all this,
place layer over layer, luminous
script over numbers over line,
and never wish to build again with brick

or block, but let the daylight break
30 through capitals and monoliths,
through the shapes that pride can make,
find a way to trace a grand design

with living tissue, raise a structure
never meant to last,
35 of paper smoothed and stroked
and thinned to be transparent,

turned into your skin.

Imtiaz Dharker

QUICK QUESTIONS

❶ What does Dharker introduce in **stanza one** that is a **recurring image** through the poem?

....

....

❷ Find a **quotation** that shows paper being treated respectfully and explain its **effect**.

Quotation: ....

....

Effect:..

....

❸ Find an example of a **simile** and explain its **impact**.

Simile: ....

....

Impact: ....

....

THINKING MORE DEEPLY

4 How does Dharker present the **concept of uncertainty** in 'Tissue'? Choose a **quotation** which illustrates this and explore its **impact**.

....

....

....

....

5 How does the **structure** of the poem help Dharker communicate her **themes**? Give **evidence** for your ideas.

....

....

....

....

....

6 Why do you think Dharker uses **imagery** of light the way she does in this poem? What is its **effect**?

....

....

....

....

....

7 What things are shown as **powerful** in this poem? Choose one and **analyse** its presentation.

....

....

....

....

EXAM PREPARATION: COMPARISON OF LANGUAGE DEVICES (A02) ✏

8 Read 'The Emigrée' by Carol Rumens. On a separate sheet of paper, write **two paragraphs** comparing the poet's use of light imagery with Dharker's in 'Tissue'. Include:

● at least one quotation from each poem which uses light imagery

● an explanation of what these quotations tell us about how light imagery is used in the poems.

PROGRESS LOG [tick the correct box]   Needs more work ☐   Getting there ☐   Under control ☐

The Emigrée

There once was a country… I left it as a child
but my memory of it is sunlight-clear
for it seems I never saw it in that November
which, I am told, comes to the mildest city.
5 The worst news I receive of it cannot break
my original view, the bright, filled paperweight.
It may be at war, it may be sick with tyrants,
but I am branded by an impression of sunlight.

The white streets of that city, the graceful slopes
10 glow even clearer as time rolls its tanks
and the frontiers rise between us, close like waves.
That child's vocabulary I carried here
like a hollow doll, opens and spills a grammar.
Soon I shall have every coloured molecule of it.
15 It may by now be a lie, banned by the state
but I can't get it off my tongue. It tastes of sunlight.

I have no passport, there's no way back at all
but my city comes to me in its own white plane.
It lies down in front of me, docile as paper;
20 I comb its hair and love its shining eyes.
My city takes me dancing through the city
of walls. They accuse me of absence, they circle me.
They accuse me of being dark in their free city.
My city hides behind me. They mutter death,
25 and my shadow falls as evidence of sunlight.

Carol Rumens

QUICK QUESTIONS

❶ What is an emigrée?

....

....

❷ What is the **impact** on the reader of **repeating the noun** *'sunlight'* at the end of every stanza?

....

....

❸ Find an example of a **metaphor** in the first stanza and explain its **effect**.

Metaphor:..

....

Effect:..

....

THINKING MORE DEEPLY

4 Choose an **image** which you find particularly striking and explain what it **implies**. How does it relate to the poem's **theme(s)**?

....

....

....

5 How does the **structure** or **form** of the poem support its message? Give **evidence** for your ideas.

....

....

....

6 In the **second stanza**, how does Rumens create a sense of the country left behind as being destroyed or in danger? Explain the **technique(s)** she uses and the **effect** created.

....

....

....

....

....

....

7 How does Rumens' use of **personification** support her **themes** in the final stanza? Give **evidence** for your ideas.

....

....

....

....

EXAM PREPARATION: COMPARISON OF THEME　A02 ✎

8 Read 'Kamikaze' by Beatrice Garland. On a separate sheet of paper, write **two paragraphs** comparing the poet's presentation of memories with Rumens' in 'The Emigrée'. Include:

- at least one quotation from each poem which shows the theme of memories
- an explanation of what these quotations tell us about how memories are presented in the poems.

PROGRESS LOG [tick the correct box]　Needs more work ☐　Getting there ☐　Under control ☐

Checking Out Me History

Dem tell me
Dem tell me
Wha dem want to tell me

Bandage up me eye with me own history
5 Blind me to me own identity

Dem tell me bout 1066 and all dat
dem tell me bout Dick Whittington and he cat
But Toussaint L'Ouverture
no dem never tell me bout dat

10 *Toussaint*
     a slave
     with vision
     lick back
     Napoleon
15   *battalion*
     and first Black
     Republic born
     Toussaint de thorn
     to de French
20   *Toussaint de beacon*
     of de Haitian Revolution

Dem tell me bout de man who discover de balloon
and de cow who jump over de moon
Dem tell me bout de dish ran away with de spoon
25 but dem never tell me bout Nanny de Maroon

Nanny
see-far woman

of mountain dream
fire-woman struggle
30 *hopeful stream*
    to freedom river

Dem tell me bout Lord Nelson and Waterloo
but dem never tell me bout Shaka de great Zulu
Dem tell me bout Columbus and 1492
35 but what happen to de Caribs and de Arawaks too

Dem tell me bout Florence Nightingale and she lamp
and how Robin Hood used to camp
Dem tell me bout ole King Cole was a merry ole soul
but dem never tell me bout Mary Seacole

40 *From Jamaica*
    she travel far
    to the Crimean War
    she volunteer to go
    and even when de British said no
45 *she still brave the Russian snow*
    a healing star
    among the wounded
    a yellow sunrise
    to the dying

50 Dem tell me
    Dem tell me wha dem want to tell me
    But now I checking out me own history
    I carving out me identity

John Agard

QUICK QUESTIONS

❶ What **technique** is Agard using in writing *'dem'* and *'me eye'* (4)?

....

....

❷ Find an example of a **metaphor** to describe Toussaint. What is its **effect**?

....

....

❸ Why do you think Agard lists nursery rhymes and legends as well as events and people from traditional British history?

....

....

THINKING MORE DEEPLY

4 Complete the table below by identifying the **technique** and the **effect** of the quotations.

Quotation	Technique	Effect
'Bandage up me eye ... Blind me' (4, 5)		
'carving out me identity' (53)		

5 What is the **impact** of using a different **form** for the Caribbean-themed stanzas?

....

....

....

....

6 How does Agard's use of **rhyme** support his **theme**? Give **evidence** for your ideas.

....

....

....

....

EXAM PREPARATION: COMPARISON OF THEME (A02) ✏

7 How would you describe the way in which the speaker **expresses** his Caribbean **identity** in the poem? On a separate sheet of paper, write **two paragraphs** exploring **two** of the following:

- how he presents Caribbean historical figures
- his views on his history education
- how he represents himself as a Caribbean individual.

PROGRESS LOG [tick the correct box]   Needs more work ☐   Getting there ☐   Under control ☐

Kamikaze

QUICK QUESTIONS

1 What **viewpoint** is used in the poem?

....

....

2 Find an example of a **simile** in the second stanza and explain its **effect**?

Quotation: ....

....

Effect: ....

....

3 Briefly describe why the **speaker** thinks the pilot returned home.

....

....

....

....

THINKING MORE DEEPLY

4 Complete the table below by identifying the **technique** and the **effect** of the examples.

Example	Technique	Effect
Line 12		
Lines 16, 17		

5 Why is the end of the fifth stanza a **turning point**? Give **evidence** to support your ideas.

....

....

....

....

6 How does Garland **create distance** in the language she uses to present these events? Use **detail** in explaining your ideas.

....

....

....

....

....

....

....

EXAM PREPARATION: FOCUS ON VIEWPOINT

A02

7 How would you describe the way in which the speaker **views** her father in the poem? On a separate sheet of paper, write **two paragraphs** exploring:

● what she imagines about his past life

● how he was treated by the community.

PROGRESS LOG [tick the correct box]   Needs more work ☐   Getting there ☐   Under control ☐

Practice task

❶ First read this exam-style task:

> Compare how poets present abuse of power in 'Checking Out Me History' and in one other poem from the *Power and Conflict* poetry cluster.

❷ Begin by circling the **key words** in the **question** above.

❸ Now complete this table, noting down three or four **points of comparison** with **evidence** and the **effect each creates**:

Point (Poem 1)	Evidence/quotation and effect	Comparison (Poem 2) – evidence and effect

❹ Draft your response. Use the space below for your first paragraph(s) and then continue on a sheet of paper.

Start: *In 'Checking Out Me History' Agard shows how the speaker has been taught ...* ....

....

....

....

....

....

....

....

....

PROGRESS LOG [tick the correct box]   Needs more work ☐   Getting there ☐   Under control ☐

PART THREE: THEMES AND CONTEXTS

Themes: Social structures and power

QUICK QUESTION

1 Which poem is which? Draw a line to match the correct title to each set of keywords:

colonialism, Nanny, Robin Hood, symbolism   'Ozymandias'

name, ranked, dramatic monologue, dowry   'Checking Out Me History'

decay, irony, sneer, my works   'My Last Duchess'

THINKING MORE DEEPLY

2 How does the Duke's **language** show his obsession with **social position and power** in the poem 'My Last Duchess'?

....

....

....

....

> ### TOP TIP
>
> Relate specific language techniques to theme in your analysis. For example: *In 'My Last Duchess' the Duke's repetition of the word 'my' shows that he sees his wife as his possession, echoing Renaissance ideas about marriage.*

3 How does Blake **create sympathy** for lower-class archetypes such as *'the chimney-sweeper'* and *'the soldier'* in 'London'? Give **evidence** for your ideas.

....

....

....

....

....

....

....

....

....

....

....

....

PROGRESS LOG [tick the correct box]   Needs more work ☐   Getting there ☐   Under control ☐

Themes: Oppression and identity

QUICK QUESTIONS ✔

❶ Tick the box with the **correct answer** to each of these questions:

a) In which poem is the theme of identity explored through a mother's memories of her son?

'Exposure' ☐   'Poppies' ☐   'The Emigrée' ☐

b) In which poem is the theme of oppression explored through race and colonialism?

'London' ☐   'My Last Duchess' ☐   'Checking Out Me History' ☐

❷ Explain the **effect** of repeatedly using *'Dem'* to represent those in power in 'Checking Out Me History'.

....

....

....

THINKING MORE DEEPLY ?

❸ **Explain** how the quotations below relate to the themes of **either oppression or identity**.

Quotation from 'The Charge of the Light Brigade': *'Theirs not to reason why / Theirs but to do and die'* (14, 15)

Link to theme: ....

....

Effect: ....

....

....

Quotation from 'The Emigrée': *'I can't get it off my tongue.'* (16)

Link to theme: ....

....

Effect: ....

....

....

PROGRESS LOG [tick the correct box]   Needs more work ☐   Getting there ☐   Under control ☐

Themes: Responsibility

QUICK QUESTION ✔

1 Which poem shows us a **character** who wants the public to be **more aware of wars** in the world and is **saddened** that the public's responses are only brief?

....

....

THINKING MORE DEEPLY ?

2 What **technique** does Armitage use in the second stanza of 'Remains' to show a concern with **responsibility**? What **effect** does it have?

....

....

....

....

....

....

....

3 How does Tennyson use **language** to indicate **responsibility for the death of so many soldiers** in 'The Charge of the Light Brigade'?

....

....

....

....

....

4 What does the quotation *'to do what someone must'* (17) tell us about the photographer's **attitude to his work** in 'War Photographer'? Why has Duffy chosen this phrase?

....

....

....

....

....

> **TOP TIP** A02
>
> Write about poets' precise choices of vocabulary, e.g. why Duffy chooses the verb 'must' rather than 'should'. Thinking about other words a poet could have used (ignoring rhyme) will help you comment on the specific effect they want to achieve.

PROGRESS LOG [tick the correct box]   Needs more work ☐   Getting there ☐   Under control ☐

Themes: Attitudes to and the effects of war

QUICK QUESTIONS ✓

1 Which poems describe wartime or battlefield experiences?

....

....

2 What **attitude** to war does the community seem to have in 'Kamikaze'?

....

....

3 Which poems show the **long-term effects** of events in wartime?

....

....

THINKING MORE DEEPLY ?

4 What does the quotation *'to do what someone must'* (17) tell us about the photographer's **attitude to his work** in 'War Photographer'? Why has Duffy chosen this phrase?

....

....

....

....

....

....

....

5 How does the imagery show the mother's fear in 'Poppies'? Give evidence for your ideas.

....

....

....

....

....

....

....

6 Find quotations that match the given **attitudes to or effects of war** and complete the table.

Attitude/effect of war	Quotation	Impact
Admiration towards the soldiers in 'Charge of the Light Brigade'		
Panic in 'Bayonet Charge'		
Sense of duty in 'War Photographer'		
Inability to forget in 'Remains'		

7 How does Garland use **viewpoint** in 'Kamikaze' to show the **effects** of the pilot's decision? Give **evidence** to support your ideas.

TOP TIP (A01)

....

....

....

....

....

....

....

Always be specific about attitudes and avoid describing them just as 'positive' or 'negative'. Considering the speaker's or other characters' precise emotions about the theme will help with this, e.g. whether they feel pride, fear, anger, etc.

EXAM PREPARATION: COMPARING ATTITUDES BETWEEN POEMS (A01)

8 On a separate sheet, explain how both poets explore ideas about people's **attitudes to war** in 'War Photographer' and 'Kamikaze'. Make sure you include **two quotations** from each poet, and describe the **effect** on the reader.

PROGRESS LOG [tick the correct box]   Needs more work ☐   Getting there ☐   Under control ☐

Themes: Memory

QUICK QUESTIONS ✓

1 Which poem tells us that the speaker's memories are a *'bright, filled paperweight'*? Tick the correct box.

'Tissue' ☐

'The Emigrée' ☐

'War Photographer' ☐

2 Which two poems deal with the negative effects of memories? Tick the correct box.

'The Prelude' and 'Remains' ☐

'Ozymandias' and 'Storm on the Island' ☐

'London' and 'My Last Duchess' ☐

3 What does the title 'Remains' suggest about the theme of memories?

....

....

....

THINKING MORE DEEPLY ?

4 How does the **personified mountain** moving *'slowly through the mind'* (43) convey the theme of memory in 'The Prelude'? Give **evidence** to support your answer.

....

....

....

....

....

5 What **purpose** do you think the mother's earlier memories serve in 'Poppies'? Give **evidence** for your answer.

....

....

....

....

....

....

6 How does Rumens use **metaphor** to convey the theme of memory in 'The Emigrée'? Choose a **quotation** to support your ideas.

....

....

....

....

....

7 How does Armitage use **different techniques** to show the effect of the soldier's memories in 'Remains'? Choose **two quotations** and explain their **effects**:

Quotation	Technique	Effect

> **TOP TIP** (A01)
>
> Make sure you focus directly on the theme specified in the question. Choosing the best poem for the theme in the question is key.

EXAM PREPARATION: COMPARISON OF THEME (A01)

8 On a separate sheet, explain how both poets explore ideas about memory in 'Remains' and 'Poppies'. Make sure you include two quotations from each poet, and **describe the effect** on the reader.

PROGRESS LOG [tick the correct box]   Needs more work ☐   Getting there ☐   Under control ☐

Themes: Nature

QUICK QUESTION

1 Which poem is which? Draw a line to match the correct title to each set of key words from nature:

wizened earth, wind dives, flung spray   'Exposure'

merciless, gusts, rain, flakes, frost, ice   'Storm on the Island'

willow, moon, craggy ridge, towered   'The Prelude'

THINKING MORE DEEPLY

2 Find a **quotation** in the first twelve lines of 'The Prelude' that shows nature to be powerful. **How** does Wordsworth achieve this?

....

....

....

....

3 Choose **quotations** which show nature to be a **destructive force** in 'Storm on the Island' and 'Exposure', and explain their **effect**. Can you also identify a **technique** the poet is using in each quotation? Complete the table below.

Poem	Quotation	Technique	Effect

PROGRESS LOG [tick the correct box]   Needs more work ☐   Getting there ☐   Under control ☐

Themes: Art

QUICK QUESTION ✔

1 Tick the box with the **correct answer** to each of these questions:

a) In which poem is the theme of control hinted at through a statue of
'*Neptune,… / Taming a seahorse*' (54, 55)? Tick the correct box.

'My Last Duchess' ☐   'Ozymandias' ☐   Tissue' ☐

b) Which kinds of oral story-telling culture does Agard include as part of the
history education described in his poem? Tick the correct box.

Fairy tales and myths   ☐

Myths and folk tales   ☐

Nursery rhymes and folk tales   ☐

THINKING MORE DEEPLY ?

2 How does Shelley use the state of Ozymandias's statue to criticise him and his
desire for power? Give **evidence** to support your ideas.

....

....

....

....

3 What does the **metaphorical noun phrase** '*A hundred agonies in black and white*'
(19) tell us about the war photographer's attitude to the photographs he produces?

....

....

....

....

4 How does Dharker use **structure and form** to support the artistic theme in
'Tissue'? Give **evidence** to support your answer.

....

....

....

....

....

> **TOP TIP** A02
>
> In discussing structure and form, look beyond rhyme and rhythm to consider aspects such as repetition and sentence forms in how the poem is constructed. This is especially valid for more recent poems which may display less patterning.

PROGRESS LOG [tick the correct box]   Needs more work ☐   Getting there ☐   Under control ☐

Contexts: The Romantics and industrialisation

QUICK QUESTION ✓

1 How does Wordsworth, as a **Romantic** writer, **idealise nature** at the beginning of 'The Prelude'?

....

....

....

THINKING MORE DEEPLY ?

2 In 'London', how does the **metaphor** *'mind-forged manacles'* (8) relate to the poem's **industrial context**?

....

....

....

....

....

....

3 Complete the table below by selecting **quotations** to illustrate the aspects of Romanticism. **Explain the effect** of each one.

Poem	Link to context	Quotation	Effect
'Ozymandias'	Respect for nature		
'London'	Interest in everyday, ordinary experience		
'The Prelude'	Interest in the idea of the self and key events helping to shape it		

PROGRESS LOG [tick the correct box]   Needs more work ☐   Getting there ☐   Under control ☐

Contexts: Crimean and First World War

QUICK QUESTION ✓

1 Which poem is which? Draw a line to match the correct title to each set of keywords about war:

sabres, cannons, Cossack and Russian, six hundred   'Exposure'

saw khaki, rifle fire, threshing hare, dignity etc   'The Charge of the Light Brigade'

drooping flares, dawn, frost, the wire, nothing happens,   'Bayonet Charge'

THINKING MORE DEEPLY ?

2 How does Tennyson encourage readers to admire the soldiers rather than just criticise their leaders, as many newspapers at the time were doing? Give **evidence** for your ideas.

....

....

....

....

....

3 What **evidence** is there that 'Exposure' was written late in the First World War and not when men were just joining up to fight?

....

....

....

....

4 How does the changing **image** of the *'patriotic tear'* [7] in the **first stanza** help us understand the soldier's feelings about the First World War in 'Bayonet Charge'?

....

....

....

....

....

....

> **TOP TIP** (A02)
>
> In your responses, try to connect comments on the context of a poem to its theme, e.g. instead of stating *'Owen fought in the First World War'*, it's more effective to say *'The weariness shown by the soldiers in 'Exposure' clearly comes from Owen's personal experience in the trenches.'*

PROGRESS LOG [tick the correct box]   Needs more work ☐   Getting there ☐   Under control ☐

Contexts: The British Empire, multiculturalism and modern conflicts

QUICK QUESTIONS

1 Why is Agard's speaker *'Checking Out* [his] *History'*?

....

....

2 Which poems have wars after the Second World War as a context?

....

....

THINKING MORE DEEPLY

3 How does Agard use **language** and **style** to change the balance of respect given to Caribbean figures in the speaker's self-education? Give **evidence** to support your ideas.

....

....

....

....

....

....

4 In 'The Emigrée', why do you think Rumens is not specific about where her emigrant is from? Give **evidence** for your views.

....

....

....

....

....

5 In 'Remains', what is the **effect** of Armitage describing Iraq as *'some distant, sun-stunned, sand-smothered land'*? What **technique(s)** is used here?

....

....

....

....

PROGRESS LOG [tick the correct box]   Needs more work ☐   Getting there ☐   Under control ☐

Practice task

1 First read this exam-style task:

> Compare how poets present social power in 'London' and in one other poem from the *Power and Conflict* poetry cluster.

2 Begin by circling the **key words** in the question above.

3 Now complete this table, noting down three or four **points of comparison** with **evidence** and the **effect each creates**:

Point (Poem 1)	Evidence/quotation and effect	Comparison (Poem 2) – evidence and effect

4 Draft your response. Use the space below for your first paragraph(s) and then continue on a sheet of paper.

Start: *In 'London', Blake presents the way social power is used as a source of 'woe' to everyone, but especially to those who have little or no power ...*

....

....

....

....

....

....

....

....

....

PROGRESS LOG [tick the correct box]   Needs more work ☐   Getting there ☐   Under control ☐

PART FOUR: STRUCTURE, FORM AND LANGUAGE

Form and structure

QUICK QUESTIONS ✓

1 Which poem in the cluster uses the **dramatic monologue** form?

....

2 Which poems are written in **blank verse**?

....

3 What is the **effect** of ending every stanza with the word *'sunlight'* in 'The Emigrée'?

....

....

....

THINKING MORE DEEPLY ?

4 Which line operates as a **refrain** in 'Exposure' and what is the **effect** of this?

....

....

....

....

....

....

5 How does the **structure** of 'War Photographer' support the ideas it conveys?

....

....

....

....

6 How does Dharker use the **structure** of the poem to help communicate her **themes** in 'Tissue'?

....

....

....

....

....

....

7 How does 'Ozymandias' follow the form of a **sonnet**? How is it different from other sonnets?

....

....

....

....

....

8 In what way is line 21 from 'The Prelude' a **turning point**?

....

....

....

9 How does Agard use **form and structure** in 'Checking Out Me History' to create separation between the 'British' and 'Caribbean' stanzas? Give **evidence** for your ideas.

....

....

....

....

> **TOP TIP**
>
> Try to comment on the effect or meaning of formal or structural elements. For example: *Writing in a dramatic monologue form allows the reader to access the speaker's thoughts directly, which may create the opportunity for irony.*

EXAM PREPARATION: COMPARING FORM AND STRUCTURE **A02**

10 Explain how both poets explore ideas about identity in 'Checking Out Me History' and 'My Last Duchess'. Include:

● at least two quotations from each poem which convey ideas about identity

● an explanation of how form and structure contribute to the theme.

PROGRESS LOG [tick the correct box]   Needs more work ☐   Getting there ☐   Under control ☐

Rhyme, rhythm and sound

QUICK QUESTIONS

1 What type of **rhyme** is used in 'London'?

....

....

2 What does the **rhythm** in 'The Charge of the Light Brigade' convey?

....

....

3 Which **theme** do you think Agard's use of **dialect** supports in 'Checking Out Me History'?

....

....

THINKING MORE DEEPLY

4 What is the **effect of the part-rhymes** used by Owen in 'Exposure'? Give **evidence** for your answer.

....

....

....

....

5 Find examples of the following **sound devices** and comment on their **effect** in 'The Charge of the Light Brigade'. Complete the table.

Device	Quotation	Effect
Onomatopoeia		
Rhyme		
Alliteration		

6 How does the **rhyme** in the following quotation support the ideas in 'War Photographer': *'The reader's eyeballs prick / with tears between the bath and pre-lunch beers.'* (21, 22)?

....

....

....

....

> **TOP TIP** **(A02)**
>
> Aim to comment on the effects of rhyme schemes and metre, e.g. *'The controlled rhyme in 'My Last Duchess' perhaps echoes the control the Duke wants to have over others, including his wife.'*

7 Why do you think Agard uses **rhyme** in certain parts of 'Checking Out Me History'? Choose and **comment on quotations** in your answer.

....

....

....

....

....

8 How does Owen use **alliteration** and **sibilance** to support the themes of 'Exposure'? Give **evidence** for your ideas.

....

....

....

....

> **TOP TIP** **(A02)**
>
> Make sure that when you comment on rhyme and rhythm, it is linked to the question. If you can't make it relevant to the question, leave it out and select other features to analyse instead.

9 Why does Shelley use a **unique rhyme scheme** (for a sonnet) in 'Ozymandias'? How does this relate to his themes?

....

....

....

....

EXAM PREPARATION: COMPARING USE OF SOUND FEATURES (A02) ✎

10 On a separate sheet, explain how both poets explore ideas about the **power of time** in 'Exposure' and 'Ozymandias'. Include:

- at least **two quotations** from each poem which convey ideas about the power of time

- an **explanation** of how rhyme and/or sound help to convey the theme.

PROGRESS LOG [tick the correct box]   Needs more work ☐   Getting there ☐   Under control ☐

Voice and viewpoint

QUICK QUESTIONS ✓

① From whose viewpoint is 'Poppies' written?

....

....

② Whose viewpoint does Wordsworth use in 'The Prelude'?

....

....

THINKING MORE DEEPLY ?

③ **How** is **viewpoint** used to support the message about **power** in 'Ozymandias'?
Give **evidence** to support your ideas.

....

....

....

....

....

④ In 'Kamizake', how do the **voice shifts** contribute to the poem's commentary on
conflict?

....

....

....

....

....

....

5 How does the **third-person viewpoint** help convey the themes in 'Bayonet Charge'?

....

....

....

....

....

6 **How** does Armitage create the **soldier's voice** in 'Remains'? Offer **evidence** to support your views.

....

....

....

....

....

....

7 In 'My Last Duchess', how does Browning use the Duke's voice to help show his character? Give **evidence** for your ideas.

....

....

....

....

....

....

EXAM PREPARATION: COMPARING USE OF SOUND FEATURES (A02) ✏

8 On a separate sheet, explain how both poets use **collective viewpoints** to present their ideas in 'Storm on the Island' and 'Exposure'. Include:

- at least **one quotation** from each poem to show the use of collective viewpoints

- an explanation of the **effect** of these viewpoints on the reader.

TOP TIP (A02)

Make sure you check the voice throughout. Any change in viewpoint will be significant and worth commenting on. For example, the shifts in 'Kamikaze' are crucial.

PROGRESS LOG [tick the correct box]   Needs more work ☐   Getting there ☐   Under control ☐

Imagery

❶ Which poems use **imagery** relating to **light**?

....

....

❷ What is Agard suggesting the speaker's education has done with the **imagery** of *'Bandage'* (4) and *'Blind'* (5) in 'Checking Out Me History'?

....

....

❸ How does Heaney use **connotation** to create increasing violence in 'Storm on the Island'? Give **evidence** for your ideas.

....

....

....

....

....

❹ How does the *'kites'* **simile** in line 24 of 'Tissue' link to **themes of power and control**?

....

....

....

....

....

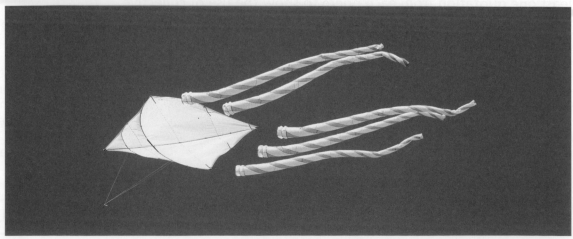

⑤ Complete the table below by identifying the **technique** used in each example and **explaining** its effect.

Poem	Example	Technique	Effect
'Poppies'	Lines 27, 28		
'Bayonet Charge'	*'cold clockwork of the stars'* (10)		
'The Prelude'	*'heaving through the water like a swan'* (20)		

EXAM PREPARATION: WRITING ABOUT IMAGERY

⑥ Read what a student has written about a **metaphor** used in 'War Photographer'. Then add a **sentence** describing the **effect** created by the metaphor.

Duffy describes the war photographer's rolls of films as 'spools of suffering', using a metaphor to label them. ....
....
....
....

> **TOP TIP** (A01)
>
> Make sure you are as specific as possible in writing about the effects of imagery. Avoid just claiming it 'helps the reader imagine' something and instead be precise, e.g. *Light imagery may symbolise hope.*

PROGRESS LOG [tick the correct box]   Needs more work ☐   Getting there ☐   Under control ☐

Poetic devices

QUICK QUESTIONS ✔

❶ Which of the poems **personifies** a mountain?

....

❷ Find an example of **ambiguity** in 'Tissue'.

....

....

THINKING MORE DEEPLY ❓

❸ Identify a **semantic field** used in the first half of the second stanza of 'The Emigrée'. What is its **effect**?

....

....

....

....

....

....

❹ Explain how **irony** is used at the end of 'War Photographer'.

....

....

....

....

....

....

> **TOP TIP** (A02)
>
> Although you may spot devices easily, it is important to make sure you link your comments about them to the question, e.g. *Hughes asks a rhetorical question in stanza two to convey the soldier's lack of control over his destiny.*

❺ How does Heaney use **personification** in different ways in 'Storm on the Island'? Give **evidence** for your ideas.

....

....

....

....

....

....

6 Complete the table below by identifying the **technique** used in each quotation and **explaining** its effect.

Poem	Quotation(s)	Technique	Effect
'The Charge of the Light Brigade'	*'Was there a man dismay'd?'* (10)		
'Exposure'	*'Pale flakes with fingering stealth come feeling for our faces'* (23)		
'My Last Duchess'	*'Even had you skill In speech – (which I have not)'* (35, 36)		
'Tissue'	*'The light'* (1), *'luminous'* (26), *'daylight'* (29)		

EXAM PREPARATION: WRITING ABOUT POETIC TECHNIQUES (A02) ✏

7 Read what a student has written about the use of irony in 'Ozymandias'. Then add a sentence describing the **effect** created by the use of irony.

Shelley shows Ozymandias's loss of power by using irony in 'Nothing beside remains'. ....

....

....

....

PROGRESS LOG [tick the correct box]   Needs more work ☐   Getting there ☐   Under control ☐

Tone and mood

QUICK QUESTION ✔

❶ Explain the **tone** of 'Exposure' in a single word or phrase.

....

THINKING MORE DEEPLY ?

❷ Which quotation signals a **turning point** in 'The Prelude's' mood? Explain how this is achieved.

....

....

....

❸ What **mood** is conveyed by the final line of 'Remains': *'His bloody life in my bloody hands'*?

....

....

....

❹ How do the **complex verb forms** in the final stanza of 'Kamikaze' contribute to the poem's **tone**?

> **TOP TIP** (A03)
>
> The tone of a poem is usually created from many different features working together, so phrases such as 'contributes to the … tone' or 'supports the … mood' are useful.

....

....

....

....

....

EXAM PREPARATION: WRITING ABOUT MOOD (A02) ✏

❺ Read what a student has written about **mood** in 'Tissue'. Then add **a sentence** describing the **effect** created by the shifts in mood.

Dharker changes the poem's mood slightly when she shifts topic with the line 'If buildings were paper'. ....

....

....

PROGRESS LOG [tick the correct box]   Needs more work ☐   Getting there ☐   Under control ☐

Practice task

❶ First read this exam-style task:

> Compare how poets present inner conflict in 'Bayonet Charge' and in one other poem from the *Power and Conflict* poetry cluster.

❷ Begin by circling the **key words** in the question above.

❸ Now complete this table, noting down three or four **points of comparison** with **evidence** and the **effect each creates**:

Point (Poem 1)	Evidence/quotation and effect	Comparison (Poem 2) – evidence and effect

❹ Draft your response. Use the space below for your first paragraph(s) and then continue on a sheet of paper.

Start: *In 'Bayonet Charge', Hughes uses imagery to present the soldier's confusion and …* ....

....
....
....
....
....
....
....
....

PROGRESS LOG [tick the correct box]   Needs more work ❑   Getting there ❑   Under control ❑

PART FIVE: COMPARING POEMS

Evaluating poems

1 Read what a student has written about the ideas in 'Poppies' and 'War Photographer'.

Specific time references such as in line 1 combined with jumps back to the son's childhood combine to create a confusing mass of memories in 'Poppies'. This contrasts with the clearer sense of recollection in 'War Photographer', where the photographer's thoughts seems as orderly as the photographs themselves in their 'ordered rows', which are echoed in the poem's form itself.

2 Which theme is being compared in the paragraph? Choose from the themes below by circling any which seem appropriate.

Time	Effects of war	Power of humans
Distance	Memory	Identity

3 What else could have been mentioned from each poem relating to the theme(s)? Write another paragraph underneath and continue on a separate piece of paper.

....

....

....

....

....

....

....

....

TOP TIP (A01)

When comparing two poems, it is important to mention both poems regularly. Writing a mini-essay on one poem and then a second on the other poem is unlikely to offer an effective or engaging comparison.

Using connectives

1 Read the following paragraphs written by a student. Circle the connectives used to **make connections** between the poems.

In 'London', Blake's exploration of power is rooted in his eighteenth-century context. This is clear in the industrial vocabulary such as the 'chimney-sweeper' and the reference to the French Revolution with the threat of 'blood' running 'down palace walls'. On the other hand, as a more modern poet, Agard writes much more directly against the system of government and education with the dismissive pronoun 'dem'.

As a result, Blake's work has a more contemplative mood, while Agard's poem has a fury to it borne of awareness of injustice. This is perhaps also linked to the poems' viewpoints, as Blake writes from the third person, but Agard's first-person perspective lends itself to a more indignant expression.

2 Select appropriate **connectives** from the box below to fill the gaps in this paragraph.

In 'Ozymandias', Shelley uses viewpoint to make the pharaoh even more powerless in the poem's time. ...., Browning creates a dramatic monologue to show the Duke's power in 'My Last Duchess'. .... poets criticise social structures in their work, ... use the perspective in the poem to do so. .... Ozymandias has lost his power over centuries, and has been reduced to a 'boundless and bare' landscape, the Duke's inability to control his wife except by violence is mirrored in his vigorous protection of his power by giving 'commands'.

and	although	however
both	unless	too
on the other hand		in the same way
while	unlike	whereas

Using quotations

1 Read what a student has written comparing 'The Charge of the Light Brigade' to 'Exposure'. Then fill in each gap with the correct quotation from the box below.

Tennyson and Owen both use repetition to show the disastrous effect of war on

soldiers. In 'Exposure', Owen uses the refrain ....

to emphasise that this is not what the soldiers would expect, and to highlight the

monotony, while Tennyson's use of ....

demonstrates how the soldiers are surrounded and outgunned. He also repeats

the phrase .... several times to draw

our attention back to the soldiers, as he wants the reader to focus on them and

their sacrifice, while Owen, writing from the trenches himself, could not have the

same goal, so he only repeats the ....

'Cannon to right of them, / Cannon to left of them,'   *'But nothing happens'*   *'nothing'*   *'six hundred'*

2 Pair up the following quotations and write them into the table below:

● Note the common theme or technique shown by each pair.

● Explain each theme or technique.

'Bandage up me eye' (4) ('Checking Out Me History')

'he sought approval / without words to do what someone must' (16, 17) ('War Photographer')

'mind-forged manacles' (8) ('London')

'myself and somebody else and somebody else' (5) ('Remains')

> **TOP TIP** **A02**
>
> When comparing, comment on form/structure/ language as well as theme. Try to compare **how** poets present ideas, not just **what** ideas they present. Choose quotations that help you do this.

Quotations	Comparison point (shared theme or technique)
Pair 1:	
Pair 2:	

Writing a comparison

1 First read the following exam-style question. Underline the most important words for answering this question effectively. You should keep the key words in mind when you write your paragraph in Question 2.

> Compare how poets present ideas about the power of nature in 'Storm on the Island' and 'The Prelude'.

You are going to write your own paragraph comparing the two poems. Use the following writing prompts to organise your paragraph:

Start with a general topic sentence beginning: *Both* …

Continue with a sentence explaining one similarity: *For example, in* …

Continue with a sentence explaining how this links to the second poem: *In the same way* …

Finish with a rounding-off sentence: *So* …

2 Write your paragraph below and continue on a separate piece of paper if you need to. Remember to include one or two quotations.

Both ……
………
………

For example, in ………
………
………
………

In the same way ………
………
………
………

So ………
………
………
………

PROGRESS LOG [tick the correct box]   Needs more work ❑   Getting there ❑   Under control ❑

Practice task

1 First read this exam-style task:

> Compare how poets present attitudes to war in 'Exposure' and in one other
> poem from the *Power and Conflict* poetry cluster.

2 Begin by circling the **key words** in the **question** above.

3 Now complete this table, noting down three or four **points of comparison**
with **evidence** and the **effect each creates**:

Point (Poem 1)	Evidence/quotation and effect	Comparison (Poem 2) – evidence and effect

4 Draft your response. Use the space below for your first paragraph(s) and then
continue on a sheet of paper.

Start: *In 'Exposure', Owen shows how the soldiers are more afraid of the weather and their
surroundings than …* ....

....

....

....

....

....

....

....

....

....

PROGRESS LOG [tick the correct box]   Needs more work ❏   Getting there ❏   Under control ❏

PART SIX: PROGRESS BOOSTER

Key skills and using quotations

1 How well can you express your ideas about the poems from the *Power and Conflict AQA Poetry Anthology*? Look at this grid and tick the level you think you are currently at:

Level	How you respond	Tick
High to Very High	• You select quotations and references very precisely and you embed them fluently in your sentences. • You analyse and explore the poets' methods and effects with detailed insight, and a thorough knowledge of poetic terminology. • You are convincing with your ideas, and offer different interpretations and perspectives. • You compare poems in a detailed and very structured way, moving fluently between ideas in the two poems	
Mid	• You support what you say with evidence and quotations. • You explain writers' methods and effects clearly, using appropriate terminology. • You show clear understanding of the main ideas and make some links between ideas. • You compare poems clearly and support your links between them.	
Lower	• You sometimes use quotations to back up what you say but they are not always well chosen, nor fluently embedded in the text. • You comment on some methods and effects, but not always using the correct terminology. • You show some basic understanding of ideas but these tend to be undeveloped. • You make some basic comparisons between the poems.	

SELECTING AND USING QUOTATIONS

2 Read these two samples from students' responses to a question about social power in 'Checking Out Me History'. Decide which of the three levels they fit best, i.e. **lower** (L), **mid** (M) or **high** (H).

Student A: *The speaker is angry at the way he has been treated. We are shown how those in power have taught him nursery rhymes as history like 'de cow who jump over de moon'. This isn't worth learning about, and nor is 'Dick Whittington' who wasn't even real. This shows how the government has wasted time on unimportant things.*

Level: ☐   **Why?** ....

....

....

Student B: *Agard uses rhyme, e.g. between 'de cow who jump over de moon' and 'de man who discover de balloon' to mock the ridiculous things that the poem's speaker has been taught. This shows his anger at how social control has been abused to enforce colonial power.*

Level: ☐   **Why?** ....

....

....

③ Which of the following quotations from the poem 'Remains' would be suitable if you were exploring the theme of the effects of war?

a) *'I see broad daylight on the other side'* (10)

b) *'the drink and the drugs won't flush him out'* (24)

c) *'dug in behind enemy lines'* (26)

④ Write a sentence explaining why:

....

....

⑤ Here is the first part of another student response to a question about 'War Photographer'. Find a suitable quotation from stanza two of the poem to fill the gap. Then explain what the quotation reveals or its effect.

When the war photographer is back home, the speaker describes England as having ...., which shows how his attitude to home has changed because of his experiences observing war. This reveals a ...

....

....

USING QUOTATIONS TO COMPARE

⑥ Here are two quotations from different poems about identity:

'I am branded by an impression of sunlight' (8) 'The Emigrée'

'a nine-hundred-years-old name' (33) 'My Last Duchess'

Complete this paragraph using the quotations to make a comparison and embedding them fluently:

When Rumens writes ...., it conveys

the idea that ....

...

However, in 'My Last Duchess', ...

...

PROGRESS LOG [tick the correct box]   Needs more work ☐   Getting there ☐   Under control ☐

Using structure and paragraphs effectively

Paragraphs need to demonstrate your points clearly by:

- using **topic sentences**
- focusing on **key words** from quotations
- explaining their **effect** or meaning.

1 Read this paragraph in which a student explains how Hughes presents inner conflict in 'Bayonet Charge':

> *Hughes presents inner conflict as the soldier faces a crisis when crossing the battlefield. He wonders 'In what cold clockwork of the stars and the nations' he is operating as a piece of machinery. The metaphor of the 'clockwork' here shows the lack of control the soldier feels over his destiny.*

Look at the response carefully.

- **Underline** the topic sentence which explains the main point about the soldier.
- **Circle** the word or phrase that is picked out from the quotation.
- **Highlight** or put a tick next to the part of the last sentence which explains the word.

2 Now read this paragraph by a student who is explaining how Duffy presents attitudes to war in 'War Photographer':

> *We find out about the war photographer when the poem says 'a priest preparing to intone a Mass'. This shows he is respectful towards the people affected by war whom he photographs.*

Expert viewpoint: This paragraph is unclear. It does not begin with a topic sentence to explain how Duffy presents attitudes to war and doesn't zoom in on any key words to analyse what those attitudes are or explain effects.

Now rewrite the paragraph. Start with a **topic sentence**, and pick out a **key word** or phrase to zoom-in on, then follow up with an explanation or interpretation, including any effect created.

Duffy presents the photographer's attitude to war as ....

....

....

....

....

LINKING IDEAS WITHIN A POEM

It is important to show your ideas are fully developed by referring to different parts of a poem.

❸ Read this paragraph by a student writing about the theme of family in 'Poppies':

> *Weir presents the mother and son in 'Poppies' as strongly connected through their many shared memories, spread over a long period of time. One tender moment is shown in line 4, where the mother fastens a paper poppy to her son's jacket/blazer. This action evokes the mother's care for the son. Later, she resists her desire to show similar tenderness (line 14), as she realises that he has grown up too much for such gestures.*

Look at the response carefully.

● **Underline** the topic sentence which introduces the main idea.

● **Circle** the first example used.

● **Highlight** the sentence which signals a link to another part of the poem.

● **Tick** any words or phrases that show these links in ideas such as 'who', 'when', 'as', 'implying', 'which', etc.

❹ Read this paragraph by another student about attitudes to conflict in 'The Charge of the Light Brigade':

> *In 'The Charge of the Light Brigade', the soldiers are shown as brave. They do not give up even though not many of them are going to survive the battle. They go into the 'valley of Death'. This shows they know they will die. They go into it anyway. The attitude they show is brave and the poem is telling us how we should celebrate them because of this.*

Expert viewpoint: The candidate has shown an understanding of the poem's message. However, the paragraph is rather awkwardly written. It needs improving by linking the sentences with suitable phrases and joining words such as 'where', 'in', 'as well as', 'who', 'suggesting', 'implying'. It also needs a further linking point added at the end to another part of the poem.

Rewrite the **paragraph**, improving the **style**, and also try to add a **further sentence** which links to another part of the poem or aspect.

Start with the same idea in your **topic sentence**, but improve it:

Tennyson gives us a vivid picture of the soldiers ....

....

....

....

....

PROGRESS LOG [tick the correct box]   Needs more work ❑   Getting there ❑   Under control ❑

Making inferences and interpretations

WRITING ABOUT INFERENCES

You need to be able to show you can read between the lines, and make inferences, rather than just explain more explicit 'surface' meanings.

1 Read this paragraph about nature from the poem 'The Prelude':

> *The speaker's understanding of nature is shown to change in the poem. We see this in the shift in tone of his descriptions, which starts with pretty imagery such as 'small circles glittering idly'. This may be beautiful but reveals his sense of purposelessness in nature's beauty at this point.*

- **Underline** the topic sentence that introduces the main idea.
- **Circle** the sentence that develops the first point.
- **Highlight** the sentence that shows inference and begins to explore wider interpretations.

2 Here are two lines from the poem 'Remains': *'One of my mates goes by / and tosses his guts back in his body'* (14, 15)

Which one of the following is an **inference** you could draw from the lines? Tick your choice:

a) His mate hasn't killed before.

b) His mate doesn't feel as affected as he does.

c) His mate is a paramedic.

Why? Write a sentence explaining why this is an appropriate inference.

....

....

INTERPRETING – YOUR TURN!

3 Now complete this **paragraph** about conflict with society as shown in the poem 'Kamikaze'. Add your own final sentence which makes inferences or explores wider interpretations:

In 'Kamikaze', ...

....

....

....

....

PROGRESS LOG [tick the correct box]   Needs more work ☐   Getting there ☐   Under control ☐

Writing about context

EXPLAINING CONTEXT

When you write about context you must make sure that what you write is relevant to the task.

Read this comment by a student about **conflict** in 'Storm on the Island':

> *In 'Storm on the Island', the storm is a metaphor for the violence that was beginning to spring up at that time among groups with different political and religious beliefs in Northern Ireland. Heaney hints at this by burying the name of the Northern Ireland parliament building, Stormont, in the title.*

① Underline the **main contextual point** made in the paragraph.

YOUR TURN!

② Now read this further paragraph in the student's response, and complete it by choosing a suitable point related to context, selecting from a), b) or c) below.

> *The community's ability to withstand the conflict around them is the poem's main theme, expressed through the extended metaphor of the storm which attacks them in increasingly violent ways. The poem's symbolic reference to the conflict around Heaney at the time of writing is most evident in ...*

a) *the simile 'like a tame cat turned savage', which shows how people once trusted can turn against you*

b) *the militaristic semantic field of verbs which increase in violence through the poem: the wind at first 'pummels' their houses, and eventually 'strafes' and 'bombard[s]' them*

c) *the personification of the sea as 'no company', suggesting people felt isolated*

③ Now write a comparison paragraph about how Owen also uses his personal experience of conflict in 'Exposure' and the effect this has on the reader (for example, his unusual perspective on war in the trenches).

....

....

....

....

....

....

PROGRESS LOG [tick the correct box]   Needs more work ☐   Getting there ☐   Under control ☐

Tackling exam tasks (A01) (A02)

DECODING QUESTIONS

It is important to be able to identify **key words** in exam tasks and then quickly generate some ideas.

1 a) Read this task and notice how the **key words** have been underlined.

Question: <u>Compare</u> how writers <u>present ideas</u> about <u>loss of power</u> in 'Ozymandias' and <u>one other poem</u> in the cluster.

b) Now do the same with this task, i.e. underline the **key words**:

Question: **Compare how writers present ideas about inner conflict in 'The Prelude' and one other poem from the cluster.**

GENERATING IDEAS

2 Now you need to generate ideas quickly. Remember, you are discussing **two poems**. Use the spider-diagrams* below and add as many ideas of your own as you can:

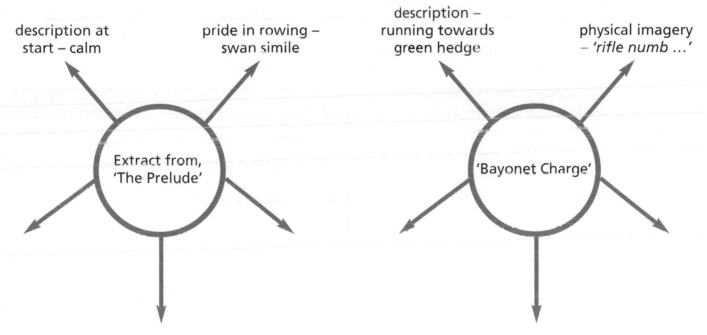

description at start – calm

pride in rowing – swan simile

Extract from, 'The Prelude'

description – running towards green hedge

physical imagery – 'rifle numb …'

'Bayonet Charge'

*You can do these as lists if you wish.

PLANNING AN ESSAY

3 **Using the ideas you generated,** write a simple **plan** with **four key points on the first poem,** and four points on the second (the first two have been done for you).

Check back to your spider diagrams or the lists you made. This structure deals with the poems in two halves of the essay – but alternatively, if you prefer, you could link and contrast points a), points b), etc. as you write the essay, moving from one poem to the other and back again.

Introduction: Brief recap of 'story' of poems and focus of task	
First half of essay: 'The Prelude'	**Second half of essay: 'Bayonet Charge'**
a) *The speaker seems happy at the start of the poem but there is a hint of trouble to come.*	a) *Similarly, the poem starts with clarity of purpose, with the soldier heading for a goal.*
b) *When he first takes the boat he is pleased with himself and proud of his rowing, taking pleasure in his own skill.*	b) *Hughes introduces physical discomfort straight away to throw some confusion into the picture.*
c)	c) ....
d)	d) ....
Conclusion:	

4 Now list at least **four quotations** for each poem (these can be single words or phrases) one for each point. The first two have been provided for you:

First poem: 'The Prelude'	Comparison poem: 'Bayonet Charge'
Quotations I could use:	Quotations I could use:
a) *'troubled pleasure'*	a) *'towards a green hedge'*
b) *'like a swan'*	b) *'numb as a smashed arm'*
c)	c) ....
d)	d) ....

5 Now read this task and **write a plan of your own**, including **quotations**, on a separate sheet of paper.

Question: Compare how writers present ideas about the power of memory in 'The Emigrée' and one other poem from the cluster.

PROGRESS LOG [tick the correct box]   Needs more work ☐   Getting there ☐   Under control ☐

Sample answers (A01) (A02) (A03)

OPENING PARAGRAPHS

Here is the task from the previous two pages.

Question: Compare how writers present ideas about inner conflict in 'The Prelude' and one other poem from the cluster.

Now look at these two alternative openings to the essay.

Student A:

> *In both 'The Prelude' and 'Bayonet Charge', writers present inner conflict. Wordsworth, in 'The Prelude', introduces a speaker who has a moment of crisis when his view of nature is challenged, creating 'a darkness' in his thoughts. On the other hand, Hughes' presentation of inner conflict is more concentrated in 'Bayonet Charge', where we witness a soldier's momentary indecision on the battlefield as he questions his place in the 'clockwork of the stars' but then quickly regains renewed energy to move forward, driven on not by patriotism but terror.*

Student B:

> *In 'The Prelude' the boy's conflict is about his views on nature as he really admires it at first, seeing it as beautiful. This view is challenged in the poem when he is frightened by the power of nature for the first time, so he experiences inner conflict over how he feels about nature. This is similar to 'Bayonet Charge', where the soldier's conflict is about why he is fighting in the war as he starts off being patriotic and really believing in the war but he has a crisis and questions everything. In the end he fights anyway because he is so scared and will die if he just stands there, like the hare.*

A good opening paragraph will:

- briefly and **concisely introduce** the 'story' of the two poems and how they interrelate
- relate the poems to the focus of the **task**
- if space allows, include brief **quotations** to help 'set the scene' for the essay.

1 Which of these two openings does this? A or B?

2 Mark or **annotate the skills** shown in the better opening paragraph (for example, concise reference to the 'story' of the poem).

3 Now it's your turn. Write the opening paragraph to the following task on a separate sheet of paper.

Question: Compare how writers present ideas about the effects of war in 'The Charge of the Light Brigade' and one other poem from the cluster.

Remember:

- **Introduce the topic** in general terms, concisely mentioning the poems' stories.
- **Explain** or 'unpick' the **key words** or **ideas** in the task (such as the theme or key idea mentioned).
- Include at least one brief **quotation** (from at least one poem) linked to the focus.
- Use the **poets' names**.

BODY PARAGRAPHS

Here are two main paragraphs in response to the question on page 77 about inner conflict. These focus on the techniques used by the poet and their effects.

Student A:

> *At the start of the poem there is a hint that all is not necessarily well because Wordsworth says that taking the boat was 'an act of troubled pleasure'. This shows that the boy has a little bit of conflict about stealing the boat maybe and hints that because of this theft there may be a problem about to happen.*

Student B:

> *Wordsworth uses foreshadowing at the start of the poem, by describing the act of taking the boat as 'an act of troubled pleasure'. This introduces a hint of inner conflict into the theft and implies that something may go wrong. The adjective 'troubled' reduces the impact of 'pleasure', casting a shadow across it, just as the mountain will do, both literally and figuratively, later in the poem.*

④ Look again at the grid for High, Mid and Lower responses on page 69.

Which level seems to match each student's response?

Student A: ....

Why? ....

Student B: ....

Why? ....

⑤ Now, take another **aspect** of either poem 1 or poem 2 and on a separate sheet of paper write your own **paragraph**. You could **comment** on one of these aspects:

● The shift in mood in Extract from, 'The Prelude'

● The soldier's 'stuck' moment in 'Bayonet Charge'

● The end of either poem

....

....

....

....

....

....

....

....

CONCLUDING PARAGRAPHS

Your final paragraph should:

- round-off or concisely **sum up** any overall view or perspective
- touch on, or hint at, the **differences** as well as the links
- efficiently **recap** ideas without listing them again (perhaps ending with a quotation you haven't used before).

Here is an effective final paragraph comparing ideas around attitudes to conflict in 'War Photographer' and 'The Charge of the Light Brigade':

> *Both poems, then, explore and seem to recommend particular attitudes to conflict or to those who have participated in conflict. 'War Photographer' expresses frustration at the world's apathy and inability to engage with those affected by conflict, while 'The Charge of the Light Brigade', written at a very different time when media reports of war were far less frequent, acts as a memorial for those soldiers lost in the Battle of Balaclava and asks us to 'honour' them. Ultimately, differences in context – Duffy speaking to a war photographer friend, Tennyson reading newspaper reports of the battle, as well as different expectations of Victorian and twentieth-century audiences – are a key reason for differences in attitude within the poems.*

6 Now complete these tasks:

- **Underline** any sentences that provide a general summing up of both poems.
- **Circle** any points that suggest the differences between the two poems.
- **Highlight** the final 'recap' sentence which cleverly links the two poems.
- **Tick** the final quotation used.

7 Practise writing concluding paragraphs of your own applying the same techniques!

COMPARING THE POEMS

Read the following longer extract in response to the task on page 77:

Response A:

> *The boy is conflicted when he is scared by the mountain in the quotation 'The horizon's bound, a huge peak, back and huge'. This shows that he is frightened because it is huge so it scares him but earlier in the poem he was thinking how beautiful everything was so now he is confused about nature.*
>
> *The soldier is scared too and is frozen because he says 'and his foot hung like statuary in mid-stride'. This means he is like a statue so he is stuck because he is so scared and does not know what to do.*

8 What could be improved in this response? Write down three things that need changing or developing.

a) ....

b) ....

c) ....

9 Rewrite the paragraphs, making the changes you think are needed, on a separate piece of paper.

Now read this second response to the task on page 77:

Response B:

> *The boy's reaction to seeing the mountain, the 'huge peak, black and huge', shows his inner conflict because he is so confused by it that he cannot think of another word but 'huge'. This contrasts to earlier in the poem where he was making beautiful imagery like 'small circles glittering idly', which also shows his earlier attitude to nature.*
>
> *'Bayonet Charge' also shows a moment of panic due to inner conflict, where the soldier freezes on the battlefield. Hughes tells us that he pauses 'and his foot hung like Statuary in mid-stride' so he didn't even put his foot on the ground, which shows how he isn't thinking at this point due to the extreme conflict he's experiencing.*

10 In what ways is Response B better than Response A? List three aspects:

a) ....

....

b) ....

....

c) ....

....

11 Look again at the criteria table on page 69. What else would the student need to do to improve it even more?

....

....

....

....

....

12 Write your own version of the response below.

....

....

....

....

....

....

....

....

....

EVALUATING A RESPONSE

Read this sample response to the following task:

Question: Compare how writers present ideas about social power in 'My Last Duchess' and one other poem from the cluster.

'My Last Duchess' and 'London' both criticise the organisation of social power most clearly through the viewpoint and setting chosen. While Browning is focused on the institution of marriage in Victorian society, by inviting us to judge a Renaissance Duke's viewpoint, Blake explores the London of his time by using the viewpoint of a person 'wander[ing] through' the 'chartered street[s]', showing disapproval that people can be wealthy and powerful enough to 'charter' even the Thames.

In 'My Last Duchess', Browning uses the dramatic monologue form to foreground the Duke's voice. This allows him to present one view of social power, of which many readers would be critical. The Duke is characterised as a typical Renaissance aristocrat who prides himself on his 'nine-hundred-years-old name', which he describes using the noun 'gift', giving it connotations of something bestowed upon his bride for which she should be grateful. His obsession with status is further emphasised with his repetition of the verb 'stoop' when he talks about correcting his wife's behaviour. Browning chooses this verb to demonstrate the Duke's preoccupation with his social position and his perceived need to metaphorically lower himself in order to point out errors to his wife. Repeating this verb shows the Duke's insistence that 'I choose never to stoop' but also invites the reader to view the Duke in a negative light, showing Browning's effective usage of the dramatic monologue form, as even though we are reading the Duke's own words, this is not to evoke sympathy with the character's viewpoint.

Blake's use of viewpoint, on the other hand, does prompt sympathy with the perspective presented. We are encouraged to share the speaker's views on social power, accepting that divisions in society have helped to create the 'marks of weakness, marks of woe' that the narrator sees on 'every face'. Like Browning, Blake also uses repetition, but because this poem has a much stronger rhythm and rhyme (as a 'Song of Experience') it relies more heavily on such formal elements to support the views presented. For Blake generally, social inequality is a key theme, so it is more central to this poem than to 'My Last Duchess', whereas it is secondary to Browning's points about the Victorian marriage market.

Browning's concerns about marriage in the Victorian period (reflected through the Renaissance setting) mean that as well as exploring power relations between the social classes in his poem he is also highlighting those between the sexes. There is mention of a 'dowry', which compensates the man for taking the woman. The Duke feigns a lack of interest in the dowry but it is clear that social structures require this to be offered and accepted. The Duke's personal misogyny, however, is clearest in the fact that he effectively confesses to having arranged the murder of his last wife to a representative of his next wife, with no sense of inappropriacy. There is some ambiguity in 'I gave commands; Then all smiles stopped together.' but the next sentence reminds us of her death, which seems to support the idea of his 'commands' as being to have her killed. Obviously we are not given the envoy's reaction, as the dramatic monologue form is by definition one-sided, but the Duke's level of comfort in sharing this information implies that he expects no shock at his revelation and presumes to proceed with the marriage arrangements.

Blake's focus, however, is much more squarely on social class divisions and he chooses to highlight a few archetypes from lower-class London such as 'the soldier' and 'the chimney-sweeper', using the definite article to universalise rather than personalise their experiences. These particular archetypes he sets against the institutions of 'palace', representing the state, and 'church', representing religion, implying that these social structures have let down and even abused the lower classes in order to profit themselves. These references also allude to the French Revolution, of which Blake was a supporter, wishing for a similar revolution in England.

> Both poets, therefore, present clear critiques of the ways social power was organised in their time. Browning's concerns encompass gender and class, while Blake's presentation is very much class-based. Their treatment of these differences varies considerably, but in both cases, the viewpoint and setting chosen is central to their message.

⑬ **Your task:**

Highlight **successful aspects** of this response. For example, **underline** or **circle**:

- examples of relevant points made
- any points of comparison
- clear use of paragraphs to move between the poems
- relevant and fluent use of quotations
- any deeper or more detailed interpretations
- good overall structure – opening paragraph, main paragraphs, concluding paragraphs
- relevant reference to poetic language and devices
- relevant reference to form and structure
- relevant reference to effects created by language, form and structure
- relevant references to context

Then, check the grid on page 69 and decide which is the right level for the response. Finally, check the Answers to see if you are correct.

Further questions   (A01) (A02) (A03)

Write full-length responses to these exam-style tasks:

❶ Compare how poets present ideas about responsibility in 'Kamikaze' and one other poem from the cluster.

❷ Compare how poets present ideas about the effects of war in 'Remains' and one other poem from the cluster.

❸ Compare how poets present ideas about oppression in 'Checking Out Me History' and one other poem from the cluster.

❹ Compare how poets present ideas about nature in 'Exposure' and one other poem from the cluster.

❺ Compare how poets present ideas about loss in 'The Emigrée' and one other poem from the cluster.

PROGRESS LOG [tick the correct box]   Needs more work ☐   Getting there ☐   Under control ☐

ANSWERS

PART TWO: EXPLORING THE POEMS

Note: Answers have been provided for most tasks. Exceptions are 'Practice tasks'.

Ozymandias [pp. 8–9]

1 He was an Egyptian pharaoh (Ramses II) whose broken statue had just been discovered and was being brought to the British Museum.

2 'Look on my works, ye Mighty, and despair!' is ironic because there is nothing left of the 'works' that Ramses/Ozymandias was boasting about.

3 **Quotation:** 'boundless and bare' (13)
Explanation: The alliteration emphasises the emptiness of this image, showing how the statue of Ozymandias is surrounded by empty desert.

4 This narrative frame shows that the story of the poem comes to us second-hand, which seems slightly disrespectful to the pharaoh, undermining his power even more.

5

Quotation	Technique	Effect
'sneer of cold command'	Alliteration	Emphasises his command.
'Look on my works, ye Mighty, and despair!'	Imperative	Shows he believes he has the right to command other rulers.

6 The imperfect sonnet form supports this. The rhyme scheme is regular but does not follow any standard sonnet pattern and there is arguably more than one volta or turning point.

7 The statement 'Nothing beside remains' (12) after the inscription from the statue is ironic by undermining the boast that Ozymandias has just made.

8 • Ozymandias is presented as arrogant through the imperative inscription on the statue: 'Look on my works, ye Mighty, and despair!'. Since this directs other rulers to 'look', it is clear that Ozymandias was not only controlling of his own people. It is perhaps ironic that his arrogance is expected to 'yet survive' when his empire and the physical manifestation of his power do not. Shelley is therefore showing how only traces of his power have lived on.
  • The Duke, however, is shown to be arrogant through his own speech, in which he proudly explains that he opts 'never to stoop'. Browning repeats the verb 'stoop', making the Duke seem preoccupied with the idea that explaining his views to his wife would equate to physically lowering himself. This, coupled with the verb 'rank' when discussing the Duchess's valuing of gifts, shows the Duke's obsession with what is his understanding of the importance of social position.

London [pp. 10–11]

1 'every'

2 **Quotation:** 'the chartered Thames' (2)
Effect: Using the adjective 'chartered' to describe the river Thames shows how ridiculous Blake finds it that wealthy people could own land and the London streets, so here he takes it to an absurd level, implying that they could even own the Thames.

3 The poem's steady rhythm helps evoke the sense of his persona walking through the streets at first. In the second stanza, the metre emphasises the repeated 'every' as the poem picks up an angrier tone.

4 The first-person narrative helps the reader to feel the same way as the speaker, as we are drawn inside the single view presented.

5 The manacles are described as 'mind-forged' to emphasise that they are sustained by people's own thoughts and beliefs – people are conditioned into feeling trapped. This is arguably the best-known image of the poem due to the impact it makes.

6 A good example of a violent image would be 'the hapless soldier's sigh / Runs in blood down palace walls', showing how the soldiers are injured and killed for the palace's benefit. The tone increases in violence as the poem goes on, perhaps because the speaker has persuaded the reader to stick with them – this is a common rhetorical technique, to start more moderately and get stronger towards the end.

7 Blake selects 'the chimney-sweeper', 'the soldier' and 'the harlot' as examples of lower-class citizens, who are the ones who suffer more from a corrupt society such as he is describing.

8 • The speaker views all the people of London as equally oppressed. This is clear from the first stanza with the statement that the speaker 'mark[s] in every face I meet / Marks of weakness, marks of woe'. This idea of everyone being equally affected continues to be emphasised in the next stanza, where the word 'every' is repeated five times to show the universal effects of the 'mind-forged manacles'. This metaphor shows how people are so oppressed that they are contributing to their own oppression by not being able to see a way out of it, so their situation has become fixed in their heads.
  • In the second half of the poem, the speaker shifts focus to specific people, presented as types rather than personalised individuals. For example, we are shown 'the chimney-sweeper', whose 'cry / Every black'ning church appalls'. Using the definite article 'the' here helps to turn this child into an archetype rather than an individual, so that the reader is aware of the church as neglecting all chimney-sweepers, not just this specific one. The metaphor of the church turning black here is a damning sign, reflecting not only the physical side of industrialisation such as soot, but also its moral angle as children were abused by having to work.

Extract from, 'The Prelude' [pp. 12–13]

1 In this poem, the speaker steals a boat for a trip out on a lake. He initially enjoys the scenery and the experience of rowing, but then a mountain appears suddenly and the speaker becomes frightened and it spoils the whole experience for him.

2 **Quotation:** 'Small circles glittering idly in the moon' (9)
Explanation: The verb 'glittering' suggests sharp beauty, while the adverb 'idly' implies that this is effortless.

3 The repetition of 'huge' shows how overcome with terror the speaker is. It leaves him unable to think clearly enough to choose another word.

4 The personification of the peak shows how Wordsworth presents nature as having a life of its own and being worthy of respect. This is shown when the peak 'Upreared its head', which is perceived as threatening by the persona and causes him to change his rowing pattern.

5 The single unbroken stanza form of 'The Prelude' contributes to the themes of memory and long-ago events still haunting the speaker, while the blank verse metric form is appropriate for storytelling. There are dramatic turning points in the extract, which are emphasised by clever use of caesura and enjambment. For example, between lines 20 and 29, caesurae and enjambment are used to control pace, delaying and speeding up events as appropriate.

6

Quotation	Technique	Effect
'elfin'	Adjective	Shows how the speaker is imagining himself into an adventure or quest, by using language more associated with the epic tradition.
'o'er my thoughts / There hung a darkness'	Metaphor	Implies the speaker's inability to forget what he has seen; shows that he is haunted by it.

7 • In 'The Prelude', the speaker's sense of nature as beautiful, protective and ultimately loving, is challenged as he encounters its darker and more destructive side. This leads to inner conflict in the form of fear and confusion as his previous assumptions are thrown into question. This is clearly demonstrated in the latter part of the poem, when the speaker describes how his 'brain / Worked with a dim and undetermined sense / Of unknown modes of being' as he is left in confusion. The adjectives 'dim' and 'undetermined' show the lack of clarity the speaker feels at this point, compared to his certainty and confidence at the start.

• In 'Remains', inner conflict is evident in the speaker's similar sense of his own brain working against him. Armitage presents the memory of the event as being in the speaker's mind against his will and against his permission: 'he's here in my head when I close my eyes'. This straightforward statement shows how much a part of everyday life it has become for the soldier, as he tells it in such a matter-of-fact way. In both poems, therefore, there is a clear sense of the speaker's mind acting against the speaker's best interests.

My Last Duchess [pp. 14–15]

1 'Dramatic monologue' means that the poem is written in a single character's voice 'in the moment', like a performance on stage.

2 The Duke controls who can see the Duchess now she is dead, in a way he could not previously, revealing the level of control that he would prefer to have over others.

3 Rhyme: couplets
Effect: This conveys the high level of control that the Duke wishes to have, although the frequent enjambments reduce the emphasis on the rhyme, perhaps suggesting that the Duke's level of self-control is quite low.

4 Browning shows that the Duke suspects everyone in relation to his wife, including 'Frà Pandolf', a man of the cloth and presumably above such suspicion. We are also given a picture of a Duchess who is pleasant to everyone, rather than untrustworthy, with her joy at being given simple gifts such as 'a bough of cherries'.

5 The emphasis on the hyphenated adjectives stressing the Duke's family lineage shows that the Duke sees power in very traditional terms. His family, as long-established aristocrats, are powerful and their name is a valuable 'gift'.

6

Quotation	Technique	Effect
'my last Duchess'	Possessive pronoun	Implies she belonged to him, while 'last' suggests she's just one in a line. She's labelled solely by her relationship to him and we do not learn anything to identify her personally.
'to make your will / Quite clear to such an one'	Tone	Makes the Duchess sound like a naughty child, while labelling her as 'such an one' is dismissive. Makes the Duchess sound like a naughty child, while labelling her as 'such an one' is dismissive.

7 • Browning shows the Duke to be controlling through the poem's form and structure. While the regular rhyming couplets show a tight control over the poem, Browning uses the metre, caesurae and enjambment to demonstrate how the Duke loses control of himself when expressing his frustrations at his 'last Duchess'. For example, when listing the things that pleased the Duchess (lines 25–31), the Duke's impatience overtakes him, resulting in long enjambments and leading up to the choppy phrases of lines 32–4: 'Somehow – I know not how – as if she ranked / My gift of a nine-hundred-years-old name / With anybody's gift.'

• This effective use of the dramatic monologue allows Browning to develop the character of the Duke as controlling and easily angered when he loses that control. The reader is able to perceive how the Duke's emotions affect him. This enables the reader to see the dramatic irony in his claims that the Duchess was unfaithful or unreliable, when we clearly see her as innocent and in fact a 'good' person who simply didn't see the danger in her husband's controlling nature.

The Charge of the Light Brigade [pp. 16–17]

1 This poem relates to the Battle of Balaclava, which was during the Crimean War.

2 The dactylic dimeter is used to imply the sound of horses' hooves.

3 The structure of the poem allows Tennyson to show readers the soldiers going into the valley and then coming back out again. This emphasises the journey the soldiers made, and the length of their ordeal.

4

Quotation	Technique	Effect
'Into the valley of Death'	Allusion (to Psalm 23)	Implies faith on the soldiers' part (as the Bible passage is about not being scared) as well as highlighting an expectation that many of them would die.
'Theirs not to make reply / Theirs not to reason why / Theirs but to do and die'	Parallel phrasing/ rhyme	Emphasises the soldiers' lack of power with the repeated 'not' and focuses on their sense of duty.

5 The listener/reader of the time would be aware of how many men were lost, so the repetition of 'six hundred' going in would remind them of how few came out of the battle.

6 Many of the verbs in this poem are strong, violent verbs. Tennyson describes the action of battle by using effective verbs such as 'storm'd' and 'thunder'd', both of which link to forces of nature, implying that the soldiers were helpless against such an onslaught.

7 • Owen presents battle itself as less terrifying than the weather. He shows how the soldiers in the First World War trenches are more frightened of the lack of change than anything else: 'We only know war lasts, rain soaks, and clouds sag stormy.' Here, Owen uses the triadic list to highlight the soldiers' experience of battle as interminable. The repeated refrain of 'But nothing happens' has a similar effect in presenting battle as a prolonged and tedious experience.

• Tennyson's presentation of battle, however, is far more active and intimidating. He begins many lines with strong dynamic verbs such as 'Flash'd' and 'Plunged', which maintains a sense of the battle as active and fast-paced. Tennyson repeats lines, as Owen does, e.g. 'Cannon to right of them, / Cannon to left of them'. The effect in this poem is very different, however, as in this case it contributes to a sense of the battle as overwhelming.

ANSWERS

Exposure [pp. 18–19]

1 The repetition of 'But nothing happens' emphasises that the soldiers might expect something to happen in war, but it continues not to happen.

2 Owen's unusual personification of the dawn shows how even aspects of nature which are usually seen as beautiful have become threatening.

3 **Quotation:** 'flowing flakes that flock' (19)
Impact: The repetition of the consonant blend in this alliteration creates a harsh and somewhat discordant effect, supporting the presentation of the snow as attacking the soldiers.

4 The plural pronoun 'Our' shows Owen's use of a communal viewpoint – this is not just his personal experience, but that of all the soldiers. Also, the present tense 'ache' creates an immediacy, so that whenever the poem is read, it appears to be happening 'now', rather than in the past.

5 Owen uses part-rhyme and near-rhyme. For example, in the first stanza 'knive us' with 'nervous' and 'silent' with 'salient'. These imperfect rhymes support his themes of frustration and monotony and offer no sense of comfort, resolution or neatness to the poem.

6 Owen states that bullets are 'less deadly than the air', showing that the temperature and the snow are the real dangers. The snow is further personified in the line 'Pale flakes with fingering stealth come feeling for our faces', implying a malicious intent to harm the soldiers.

7 The stanza about home emphasises the soldiers' desperation as they do not seem to even believe that they would be welcome back home, stating 'on us the doors are closed'. This stanza is likely to have the effect of increasing the reader's sympathy for the soldiers in their depression.

8 • Owen presents the soldiers' attitude to war as dismissive. He refers to it as 'flickering gunnery', which makes it sound relatively weak and supports the following description of it as 'Far off'. The repetition of 'But nothing happens' shows that the soldiers have become bored, highlighted by the opening 'But' to this clause which clearly indicates an expectation that something should happen. The war has become tedious and they are unable to imagine it ending.

 • On the other hand, what the soldiers are worried about is the steady assault of nature. Even dawn, usually presented as a symbol of hope, is here personified as bringing a 'melancholy army' in 'ranks on shivering ranks of grey' to attack them. This image presents an attitude of being victimised by the very weather, which is seen as deliberately aiming to injure the soldiers. The military language used here implies that it is nature itself, rather than the opposite side in the war, which is the soldiers' real enemy.

Storm on the Island [pp. 20–1]

1 'We are prepared' shows the community expects storms to happen at any time.

2 'pummels' can be seen as violent vocabulary, which Heaney might have chosen to show how the wind would hit the house repeatedly, not just once or twice.

3 Colloquial phrases such as 'as you see' help to create a conversational tone, so it feels as if the speaker is addressing the reader directly or maybe thinking aloud.

4 Lines 9–10 on a literal level could show how people can get distracted by the noise of the storm, forgetting how destructive it is. More figuratively, Heaney may be referring to the seductive nature of drama and gossip which people can get involved in without initially realising how harmful they can be.

5 Heaney uses the pronoun 'we' to present a community viewpoint. In a more symbolic reading of the poem, this encourages the reader to see the community as united against outbreaks of sectarian violence.

6

Quotation	Technique	Effect
'raise a tragic chorus'	Allusion (Greek drama) Personification	Implies that the noise from the trees would provide a warning of impending danger.
'spits like a tame cat turned savage'	Simile	Suggests that something once trusted (e.g. the sea which probably provides food) could change to become violent.

7 • In 'The Prelude', Wordsworth shows nature as threatening through personification when the peak 'Towered up between me and the stars'. This is threatening not only because the peak is frightening, but also because it symbolically blocks the boy's access to his earlier view of nature, signalling to the reader that this view is changing. This need to change his view of nature is threatening in itself to the boy, who had previously only seen nature as benevolent and pretty, but now must also reconcile a view of nature as powerful in its own right.

 • Heaney's presentation, however, is less abstract. He presents the wind associated with a storm using a military semantic field to show its power and the threat it carries. The verbs 'dives', 'strafes' and 'bombarded' and the noun 'salvo' all come from this semantic field and are used in the final four lines of the poem to show how the wind assaults the community. This choice of semantic field may also be to underline the symbolic meaning of the poem as referring not only to literal storms but also to outbreaks of sectarian violence in Northern Ireland at the time of writing in the 1960s.

Bayonet Charge [pp. 22–3]

1 'In bewilderment then he almost stopped' shows that the soldier is prevented from moving forwards by the internal conflict he is experiencing. (Other possible quotations include: 'Was he the hand pointing that second?' and 'Listening between his footfalls for the reason / Of his still running').

2 The repetition of 'raw' emphasises both that the soldier is inexperienced and the physical discomfort he is experiencing.

3 **Image:** 'Bullets smacking the belly out of the air'
Effect: This physical imagery creates the sound of the shots, but also shows how they affect the air around the soldier.

4 The 'clockwork' image shows us that the soldier feels he is just a tiny part in someone else's plan, that he does not have any control in the situation. The reference to the 'stars and nations' emphasises how much bigger than just him this all feels, while the description of the clockwork as 'cold' implies it is uncaring and emotionless.

5 Hughes evokes sight with words like 'dazzled' and colour imagery, showing how the battlefield is too bright for the soldier. At the same time, onomatopoeia such as 'smacking' is used to convey the sounds around him, and physical sensation is also richly described with the adjective 'raw' and phrase 'sweating like molten iron'. The overall effect is that it is all too much for the soldier.

6 The hare is a turning point in the poem because it acts as a warning sign and as a catalyst for the soldier to start running again. The disturbing imagery enables the reader to see how war affects nature, represented by the hare, and to understand why the soldier recognises the danger he is in and moves off once more.

7 Hughes uses the list 'King, honour, human dignity, etcetera' to suggest ideals that people have often fought for, and to show how ultimately they do not matter. The soldier, in the moment, makes the decision to fight on purely because of his terror. The dismissive 'etcetera' as well as the statement that these are 'dropped like luxuries' makes this clear.

8 • Hughes shows how the soldier felt patriotic before the war with the phrase 'The patriotic tear that had brimmed in his eye'. The tense of this clearly shows that this feeling is long past, as it 'had brimmed'. The description continues, to show how this tear has evolved: 'Sweating like molten iron from the centre of his chest'. This image highlights the progression of the soldier's feelings, from idealism to absolute terror that burns him from the inside.

• The reality of war is shown to be too bright, noisy and difficult. Even the soldier's uniform is uncomfortable with its 'raw-seam[s]' and his rifle is difficult to carry and seemingly useless, shown through the simile 'numb as a smashed arm', which implies disability The image of the hare moving 'in a threshing circle' also mirrors the reality of injured soldiers in no man's land, showing how the soldiers have had to face horrors in war.

Remains [pp. 24–5]

1 In this poem, a soldier sent to stop looters raiding a bank is involved in killing a looter. He is unable to forget the incident.

2 **Quotation:** 'legs it'
Effect: This contributes to making the poem sound like an ordinary anecdote told by an ordinary person.

3 The phrase 'blood-shadow' emphasises the staying power of the stain on the street. 'Shadow' also has metaphorical power as something negative or evil.

4 The title 'Remains' may imply: what is left of the soldier psychologically after the event; the bodily remains of the shot man; the mental replaying of the event that the soldier seems compelled to do.

5 The conversational tone helps create an impact by contrasting with the violent nature of the poem's content. It's more shocking to think of 'letting fly' as being shooting someone, when that might usually mean with words or maybe fists. Also, the colloquialisms make the voice very British, which emphasises how out of place the soldier is in a 'sun-stunned, sand-smothered land'.

6

Technique	Quotation	Effect
Idiom	'near to the knuckle'	Implies it's too close for comfort, more than the soldier can cope with.
Metaphor	'it rips through his life'	Emphasises that the bullets are killing the man.

7 • Armitage uses different ways of saying the same thing to show the reader how important it is to the speaker that 'three of us' are seen as responsible. The effect of this, however, is to suggest that recognising the involvement of three individuals

does not help to make the speaker feel less guilty. The metaphor 'rips through his life' is also used to show horror at a life being taken and the hyperbole 'I see broad daylight on the other side' to support this sense of shock at the death.

• The speaker's inability to forget is the focus of the second half of the poem, which opens with the ironic colloquialism 'End of story'. Armitage later uses irregular rhythms and sentence structures to show the way that the speaker's life is interrupted by visions of the events: 'Sleep, and he's probably armed, possibly not. / Dream, and he's torn apart by a dozen rounds.' The closing line 'his bloody life in my bloody hands' shows Armitage using 'bloody' as a mild expletive as well as in the literal sense to express the soldier's anger at what he's been left with.

Poppies [pp. 26–27]

1 The speaker in this poem is a mother whose son has left for war.

2 Weir's image in line 5 conveys pain by implying that the paper is cramping up. This suggests that the poppy is a sudden shock on his blazer.

3 **Technique:** metaphor, line 24
Effect: It makes crying seem beautiful and also gives a sense of the letting go of emotion in the act of crying.

4 The many time references allow Weir to move through different time periods, and also relate to the theme of memories, as the mother thinks about the boy's childhood as well as the immediate past.

5

Example	Technique	Effect
Lines 20, 21	Simile	Shows the possibilities available to him.
Lines 27, 28	Metaphor	Shows her nervousness in a textural image.
Lines 10, 11	Sibilance	Soft sounds show how difficult it was for her to appear strong for him and hide her softness.

6 The poem is written in stanzas of two different lengths, in two halves, using lines of around ten syllables. There are many examples of enjambment and some caesurae, making the poem flow very naturally. The lack of rigidity fits with the theme of memories, and the enjambment supports the flow of memories as they run through the poem.

7 • Viewpoint is central to both 'Poppies' and 'Kamikaze'. Weir's first-person speaker clearly addresses a second-person 'you' throughout her poem, giving the poem a warmth and sense of connection. The reader is given a sense of eavesdropping on a private conversation between a mother and son as she reminisces with him about his leaving for war. This is due to the inclusion of small, domestic details such as in lines 8–10, which feel very personal.

• 'Kamikaze', although it similarly tells a family story, does not share this sense of a private conversation intruded upon. Opening in the third person, Garland uses a more complex viewpoint to present her story. She does eventually shift to the pilot's daughter's voice, but a sense of distance is more important to the themes of 'Kamikaze'. Where personal voice is used, for example in lines 32–33, the poignancy of this straightforward statement has more impact for being used more sparingly, showing the finality of her father's situation.

ANSWERS

War Photographer [pp. 28–9]

1 'All flesh is grass' is an allusion from the Bible (Isaiah 40:6), meaning that human life is temporary.

2 **Quotation:** The photographer's respectful attitude towards his work is shown through 'as though this were a church and he / a priest preparing to intone a Mass'.
How it reveals his respectful attitude: This shows he is reverential to his work, treating it like a priest getting ready for church.

3 Writing from an omniscient perspective allows Duffy to write about the photographer from the outside but still to know his thoughts and feelings. This enables her to comment on his attitude and his frustration with other people's attitudes.

4 The photographer finds 'rural England' dull and seems a bit critical of English people. This is seen in the phrase 'ordinary pain which simple weather can dispel', which implies that people take things for granted and should be more grateful.

5

Quotation	Technique	Effect
'He has a job to do.'	Simple sentence	Emphasises his sense of duty by its brevity.
'The reader's eyeballs prick / with tears between the bath and pre-lunch beers.'	Internal rhyme	Mocks the lack of real feeling that the readers have.

6 • The war photographer approaches his work seriously. He 'set[s] out' the photographs 'in ordered rows' which is a metaphor for the self-control he has over his emotions when taking his photographs. He does not allow himself to respond emotionally when he is out in the war zones as 'his hands … did not tremble then / though seem to now'. This contrast shows how he is able to manage his emotions in front of the people he photographs and he only really thinks about it back home. This is one way he shows respect for his work, another is that he treats it like 'Mass'.

• Duffy shows the war photographer to have a sense of duty about his work. When he wants to photograph a man in pain he asks his wife's permission 'to do what someone must'. Using the verb 'must' presents the war photographer as seeing his work as crucial. The idea that only 'five or six' out of 'a hundred agonies' will be printed is presented as a juxtaposition in order to show the relatively high emotional and material cost and to contextualise the reader's disappointing response.

Tissue [pp. 30–1]

1 Dharker introduces the recurring image of paper being 'thinned' by touch in stanza one, which shows how important it will be to the poem.

2 **Quotation:** 'pages smoothed and stroked'
Effect: The paper sounds like something precious and/or loved.

3 'Fine slips from grocery shops … might fly our lives like paper kites' is a simile used to suggest that money and its management controls our lives.

4 Dharker uses uncertain language throughout the poem to show how she is writing imaginatively and tentatively. For example, in 'If buildings were paper, I might / feel their drift', both the conditional clause and the modal verb 'might' create this uncertainty and signal a shift in the poem to more abstract ideas.

5 Dharker layers the poem by repeating lines and phrases, such as 'paper smoothed and stroked and thinned', just as she says that architects could layer paper for building. In this way, the poem's form mirrors and supports its themes.

6 The repeated references to light may be seen as linking to the idea of change introduced at the start of the poem – Dharker may be suggesting a need to allow light to show where change is needed. Additionally, light is a standard symbol for hope and here its ability to go through barriers is emphasised, perhaps implying a need to break down barriers between people/nations/races. Other relevant concepts linked to light include fragility, vulnerability, beauty and (im)permanence.

7 Maps are shown to be powerful in the poem, representing borders and boundaries of different kinds. Dharker uses a list with alliteration in 'the marks / that rivers make, roads, / railtracks, mountainfolds' to connect a range of both manmade and natural lines on maps, which all seem permanent but equally all let the sun shine through.

8 • Light is seen as a powerful force in 'Tissue', often presented as more powerful than paper and the constructions represented by paper in the poem, culminating in 'let the daylight break / through capitals and monoliths'. The daylight here is presented as breaking down or showing up 'capitals and monoliths', both of which have meanings relating to the physical world and the world of ideas. Capitals may relate to letters as well as cities and a monolith might be an idea as well as a statue, thus light is seen as opening the way to new ideas or new systems of thought, not just new buildings.

• In 'The Emigrée', however, light is a more straightforward symbol of hope. This is most apparent in the repetition of the noun 'sunlight' as the final word of each stanza. Rumens uses this to emphasise the enduring nature of the emigrée's positive impression of her city. The constant association of these memories with light enables the reader to perceive a clear sense of affection associated with these memories, despite obvious darker tones to the speaker's relationship with her 'city'.

The Emigrée [pp. 32–3]

1 An emigrée is a female migrant who has moved away from somewhere.

2 Repeating the noun 'sunlight' at the end of every stanza leaves the reader with a clearly positive impression of the speaker's memories.

3 **Metaphor:** 'the bright, filled paperweight'
Effect: Shows the value of the speaker's memories and associates them with beauty and fragility

4 Rumens' simile, 'like a hollow doll', shows how the speaker's grasp of the language was fragile and undeveloped and the use of 'doll' links it firmly to her as a child.

5 The poem's measured tone and controlled stanzas – all end-stopped and even ending with the same word – support the sense of having to be controlled in the new country.

6 Rumens creates a sense of the country left behind as being destroyed or in danger in the second stanza, using a military semantic field with 'tanks' and 'frontiers' at the beginning of the stanza to imply danger, although this usage is metaphorical. Towards the end of the stanza, she more clearly presents a sense of her former country as in danger through references to its language being wiped out or 'banned by the state', which suggests a repressive regime.

7 Rumens' use of personification in the final stanza creates a sense of her city as a character. In this stanza, the city appears like a pet at first, which 'lies down in front of me, docile as paper' for her to pet and groom, but then the presentation shifts to more like a lover with 'My city takes me dancing'. These characterisations are used to contrast with the city she lives in, which accuses her of 'being dark', showing how she doesn't belong or is seen as an outsider.

8 • In 'Kamikaze', memories are presented as possibly an influence on the pilot, which made him turn back and abandon his mission. The pilot getting lost in the memory and so making the decision to turn back and return home is reflected in the list of fish caught by his father (lines 27–30). The length of this list, and amount of detail given about the fish caught by his father when he was a boy shows how the pilot gets caught up in his memories and therefore how this has the power to make him turn back home.

• In 'The Emigrée', similarly, memories are shown to be powerful emotionally. The speaker reports that she is 'branded by an impression of sunlight'. This metaphor implies that the sense of sunlight which the speaker retains from her home city is burnt into her – a memory at once beautiful, powerful and somewhat painful.

Checking Out Me History [pp. 34–5]

1 Agard is using phonetic spelling to represent Caribbean dialect.

2 Toussaint is described as a 'thorn' to the French, showing how he constantly bothered them, like the idiom 'thorn in my side'.

3 Agard lists nursery rhymes and legends as well as traditional British history to show how time was wasted learning unimportant/untrue things that could easily have been spent on Caribbean history.

4

Quotation	Technique	Effect
'Bandage up me eye ... I Blind me'	Semantic field of visual impairment; Alliteration	Shows how the system is disabling the speaker by not allowing him to know his own heritage
'carving out me identity'	Metaphor	Shows the speaker reclaiming himself actively, using image of a sculptor.

5 Using a different form for the Caribbean-themed stanzas gives them a different tone. They seem more lyrical, while the British-themed stanzas use stricter rhythms, supporting an idea of Caribbean identity as more free-flowing and less restrictive.

6 Agard's uses more rhyme, which is often simple and childish, in the British-themed stanzas. For example, rhyming 'balloon', 'moon', 'spoon' and 'maroon' all in one four-lined stanza feels deliberately excessive.

7 • Agard presents the Caribbean historical figures in the poem with affection and respect, saving the most lyrical and beautiful poetic expressions for them. These sections of the poem all include imagery relating to light, which shows how Agard wants to present these figures as symbols of hope for the future. This starts with 'Toussaint de beacon', continues with 'fire-woman' for Nanny the Maroon and closes with depicting Mary Seacole as 'a yellow sunrise'.

• The history education received in the Caribbean is presented as damaging and absurd. The metaphors 'Bandage up me eye with me own history' and 'Blind me to me own identity' show how Agard presents the speaker as being disabled by the education he has been given, which has not allowed him to fully understand his roots as a Caribbean.

• Using dialect to represent the speaker as a Caribbean individual, Agard begins straight away to 'carv[e] out me identity' through the act of writing. By using dialect forms such as 'dem' and 'me', he is centring the Caribbean dialect on the page and giving it the legitimacy which the poem shows has been denied to Caribbean identity in the school curriculum.

Kamikaze [pp. 36–7]

1 This poem is told initially from a third-person viewpoint, which switches to that of the pilot's daughter part-way through.

2 Example: Lines 10, 11
Effect: Implies celebration and is an image of simple beauty.

3 The speaker thinks the pilot returned home because everything he saw made him want to live, reminding him of his family and his childhood in particular.

4

Example	Technique	Effect
Line 12	Colour imagery	Emphasises the clarity of the water and beauty of nature.
Lines 16, 17	Alliteration	Sounds evoke the quick movements of the fish.

5 The end of the fifth stanza is a turning point because this seems to be where the pilot's mind was made up. In more formal terms, this first full stop of the poem marks a shift in voice, as the pilot's daughter speaks after this.

6 Garland creates distance primarily using viewpoint. The poem is largely told in the third person by an unconnected speaker who relates the story, seeming to focus on the pilot's daughter rather than on him directly (adding to the distance). Then when we do shift to the daughter, as she hadn't spoken to her father since his return, it isn't any more 'first-hand' a narrative than anyone else's telling of it, so she has to imagine what he thinks/feels, leading to complex verb phrases such as in lines 41–42.

7 • The speaker imagines her father's thoughts and feelings while flying his kamikaze mission. She believes that he must have been influenced by what he saw from his plane and that this must have triggered childhood memories. She describes his memory of waiting for his father to return from fishing (line 24), and this seems to be the catalyst for his return, suggesting that she sees him as a loving father. The repetition in lines 24 and 25 implies that this is what the daughter sees as her father's key memory – the idea of awaiting his own father's safe return.

• When he did return, the daughter notes that everyone 'treated him / as though he no longer existed' and that the children took longer to learn this behaviour. There is a sense of regret in the poem's final stanza, in its convoluted musings about the father's thoughts and feelings on the situation.

PART THREE: THEMES AND CONTEXTS

Theme: Social structures and power [p. 39]

1 colonialism, Nanny, Robin Hood, symbolism – 'Checking Out Me History'
name, ranked, dramatic monologue, dowry – 'My Last Duchess'
decay, irony, sneer, my works – 'Ozymandias'

2 The Duke's use of the verb 'ranked' in discussing how his Duchess viewed her 'gifts' shows his obsession with social position and power because it demonstrates that he sees everything in those terms. He cannot understand that the Duchess does not operate in the same way.

3 Blake creates sympathy for lower-class archetypes such as 'the chimney-sweeper' and 'the soldier' by showing their oppression at the hands of corrupt institutions. In both these cases, the archetypal labels are followed by the nouns 'cry' or 'sigh', showing how these types are responding to their treatment.

Themes: Oppression and identity [p. 40]

1 a) 'Poppies' b) 'Checking Out Me History'

2 Repeatedly using 'Dem' to represent those in power in 'Checking Out Me History' is one way that Agard's speaker is trying to claim back his power and identity.

3 **Quotation from 'The Charge of the Light Brigade':** 'Theirs not to reason why / Theirs but to do and die' (14–15)
Link to theme: Oppression
Effect: Shows how the soldiers have no choice but to follow even badly-thought-out commands.
Quotation from 'The Emigrée': 'I can't get it off my tongue.' (16)
Link to theme: Identity
Effect: Shows how her original language is part of her and always will be.

Theme: Responsibility [p. 41]

1 'War Photographer'

2 Armitage uses repetition of the idea that there were three shooters in the second stanza of 'Remains' to show a concern with responsibility. This demonstrates the speaker's feelings of guilt, as he emphasises this point by re-stating it four different ways, but he still can't shake the feelings of responsibility for the man's death.

3 Tennyson directs responsibility with the phrase 'Some one had blunder'd'. This shows a clear sense that an individual was responsible for the disastrous battle, but Tennyson, as Laureate, was not in a position to apportion blame clearly and directly.

4 The quotation 'to do what someone must' shows the reader that the photographer sees his work as vital. This type of phrase has sometimes been associated with patriotic duty such as going to war, so its usage here is interesting as the importance in this context is about making people aware of world events, rather than fighting for a country.

Theme: Attitudes to and the effects of war [pp. 42–3]

1 'The Charge of the Light Brigade', 'Exposure', 'Bayonet Charge', 'Remains', 'Poppies', 'War Photographer', 'Kamikaze'

2 The community in 'Kamikaze' seems to have a positive attitude to war in that they see it as a necessary thing to participate in and a disgrace to back out of.

3 'Remains', 'Kamikaze'

4 The personification of the weather helps Owen show the soldiers' attitude to the war by contrasting their fear of the weather with their nonchalant attitude to the battle going on around them. This is clear in the fourth stanza, when the bullets are described using sibilance to emulate their whistling sound: 'Sudden successive flights of bullets streak the silence' but their power is reduced by the next line 'Less deadly than the air'.

5 Imagery of textures and textiles is used to show the mother's fear in 'Poppies', for example in lines 27–28. This metaphor clearly shows the metaphorical physical movements of the mother's stomach in interesting textile-related terms.

6

Attitude/effect of war	Quotation	Impact
Admiration towards the soldiers in 'Charge of the Light Brigade'	'Noble six hundred!'	Shows how the speaker feels we should see the Light Brigade.
Panic in 'Bayonet Charge'	'king, honour, human dignity etcetera / Dropped like luxuries'	Reveals that the reasons people sign up for war lose meaning in the heat of battle.
Sense of duty in 'War Photographer'	'He has a job to do'	Demonstrates the war photographer's professionalism.
Inability to forget in 'Remains'	'And the drink and the drugs won't flush him out'	Conveys the desperation the soldier has been feeling.

7 Garland uses the pilot's daughter's viewpoint in 'Kamikaze' to show how the pilot's decision had long-term effects. Using this viewpoint in addition to the external third-person narrator at the start allows Garland to show how the pilot's decision impacted on the next generation, as the children learnt only slowly how they were supposed to act to fit in with the community's code.

8 • In 'War Photographer', Duffy explores different attitudes to war using the speaker and his audience. The photographer himself shows concern for those he photographs, treating his 'spools of suffering' with a high level of respect and holding his own role in high reverence, seeing it as doing 'what someone must'. On the other hand, the people who look at his photographs are only momentarily affected and Duffy shows their trivial response using internal rhyme in 'The reader's eyeballs prick / with tears between the bath and pre-lunch beers.' This rhyme shows how short-lived the 'tears' are and therefore how low-priority the suffering of others is to the reader.

• In 'Kamikaze', on the other hand, we are shown a community shunning a member for not carrying out his mission, demonstrating that their attitude to war is very serious. Garland presents the pilot initially as though he were under a spell (lines 4, 5), suggesting that the propaganda given to kamikaze pilots was hard to resist. At the end of the poem, though, when the pilot has returned, the children are made to understand that their father has changed (lines 39, 40). This declarative presents this idea as a fact which the children had to learn, showing the clear attitude that war and serving in the war was all-important.

Theme: Memory [pp. 44–5]

1 'The Emigrée'

2 'The Prelude' and 'Remains'

3 The title 'Remains' evokes the memories that the soldier is left with – the scene is lodged in his brain and will not shift.

4 The personified mountain moving 'slowly through the mind' shows how the boy is unable to forget. His traumatic experience, encountering nature's darker side, has left him haunted by what he saw.

5 The mother's earlier memories help to create a sense of her relationship with her son. It also supports the theme of memory to have the speaker remember other times that link. For example, when she says goodbye to her son to go to war, it is natural that she would reminisce about him starting school.

6 Rumens uses metaphor to support the theme of memory with the imagery of the speaker's former language. She refers to 'every coloured molecule' of this language, which implies that the language is bright and complex, while the metaphor 'I can't get it off my tongue' suggests that she is unable to let go of this language, even if she wants to.

7

Quotation	Technique	Effect
'Sleep, and he's ... / Dream and he's ...' (22, 23)	Repeated structure	Portrays how the memories constantly interrupt his everyday life, replaying themselves.
'his bloody life in my bloody hands' (30)	Mild expletive Double meaning Repetition	Shows his frustration that he can't stop thinking about the killing.

8 • In 'Remains', Armitage presents memory as a problem to the soldier who is haunted by memories of a traumatic experience, while in 'Poppies', Weir presents a speaker who finds comfort in her memories of a son who has gone to war.

• In 'Remains', Armitage shows how the soldier cannot escape the memories of the events even when back at home. He uses sentence structure to show how the looter breaks into the soldier's mind: 'But I blink / and he bursts again through the doors of the bank. / Sleep, and he's probably armed, possibly not. / Dream, and he's torn apart by a dozen rounds.' These sentences, all headed with the soldier's simple daily actions of 'blink', 'sleep', 'dream', show how the speaker feels that his mind is invaded by these memories.

• Weir, on the other hand, presents memories interspersed with the action of the poem, creating a complex timeline that shows how the mother is perhaps living in confusion as she is so worried for her son. A description of getting the son ready to leave is interrupted by a memory of 'play[ing] at / being Eskimos like we did when / you were little' and the poem closes with a reference to 'your playground voice', which the reader is left to assume the mother used to hear when he was younger.

Theme: Nature [p. 46]

1 wizened earth, wind dives, flung spray – 'Storm on the Island'
merciless, gusts, rain, flakes, frost, ice – 'Exposure'
willow, moon, craggy ridge, towered – 'The Prelude'

2 'Small circles glittering idly in the moon' shows nature to be powerful by highlighting its beauty and effortlessness.

3

Poem	Quotation	Technique	Effect
'Storm on the Island'	'exploding comfortably'	Oxymoron	Presents sea as frightening when it's normally safe and welcoming.
'Exposure'	'merciless iced east winds that knive us'	Sibilance	Shows nature as attacking them; sense of wind as being so cold it feels like a knife.

Theme: Art [p. 47]

1 a) 'My Last Duchess' **b)** Nursery rhymes and folk tales

2 Shelley uses the state of Ozymandias's statue to show how, despite his extreme wealth and power, his empire still crumbled

both literally and figuratively eventually. This is clear from the start with the juxtaposition of 'vast and trunkless' showing both the immense size and broken nature of the statue in its immediate introduction.

3 The metaphorical noun phrase 'A hundred agonies in black and white' tells us that the war photographer sees his photographs as pieces of history and not just images. He clearly sees what is represented rather than just the image.

4 Dharker uses repetition throughout 'Tissue' to support what she says about the architect and the construction of beauty. Where she writes about layering she demonstrates this idea with the words and phrases she chooses: 'place layer over layer, luminous / script over numbers over line'. Here, the repetition of 'over' mirrors the idea outlined in the words and reinforces the concept of layers.

Contexts: The Romantics and industrialisation [p. 48]

1 Wordsworth idealises nature at the beginning of 'The Prelude' by presenting it in a personified female form and using only imagery which emphasises its effortlessness and beauty.

2 The famous metaphor 'mind-forged manacles' relates to the poem's industrial context by emphasising the physical construction of the manacles, implying that they are 'forged', or made by a blacksmith. This suggests a lengthy and skilled process requiring careful working of the metal using heat and a range of tools.

3

Poem	Link to context	Quotation	Effect
'Ozymandias'	Respect for nature	'the lone and level sands stretch far away'	Shows how nature is the thing that endures, not human power.
'London'	Interest in everyday, ordinary experience	'I wander through each chartered street'	Demonstrates concern for whole of city and issues affecting ordinary people.
'The Prelude'	Interest in the idea of the self and key events helping to shape it	'no familiar shapes / Remained'	Shows after-effects of the incident – it changed everything and how he saw things from then on.

Contexts: Crimean and First World War [p. 49]

1 sabres, cannons, Cossack and Russian, six hundred – 'The Charge of the Light Brigade'
raw khaki, rifle fire, threshing hare, dignity etc – 'Bayonet Charge'
drooping flares, dawn, frost, the wire, nothing happens – 'Exposure'

2 Tennyson encourages readers to admire the soldiers rather than just criticise their leaders by focusing on their bravery. He shows that they knew what they were facing by going 'Into the valley of Death', but this biblical allusion implies that they were not afraid. He also foregrounds how many of them were lost, to increase readers' pity, with the repetition of 'six hundred' and its emphasis through the rhyme with words such as 'blunder'd' and 'thunder'd'.

3 'Exposure' was clearly written late in the First World War because of the mood shown in the poem. The desperation and despondency of 'But nothing happens' can only come after a prolonged period of fighting.

4   The image of the 'patriotic tear' shows the reader how the soldier initially felt moved by patriotism – to the point of tears. At the point of the poem's action, however, this emotion has shifted to 'molten iron from the centre of his chest', revealing a shift from a somewhat disconnected, idealistic emotion to something much more real and painful.

Contexts: The British Empire, multiculturalism and modern conflicts [p. 50]

1   Agard's speaker is 'Checking Out [his] History' to fill the gaps in his knowledge that resulted from his education being focused on British history.

2   'Poppies', 'War Photographer', 'Remains', 'The Emigrée'

3   Agard grants the Caribbean figures more respect in his poem through metaphor and a more lyrical style, e.g. 'Nanny / see-far woman / of mountain dream'. This feels almost dream-like in its presentation and clearly connects the figure of Nanny to nature and idealism through the phrase 'mountain dream'.

4   Rumens is not specific about where her emigrée is from, perhaps in order to explore the idea of being away from one's country rather than getting caught up in the details of one particular place. This also allows her to remain free of politics and the reader to be neutral in relation to 'my country' and 'my city' – if it were set in any real place, people could always already have particular views.

5   Armitage uses sibilance to describe Iraq as 'some distant, sun-stunned, sand-smothered land'. This softens the phrase, which is quite distancing and dismissive of the country, showing the soldier's unpleasant associations and negative memories.

PART FOUR: STRUCTURE, FORM AND LANGUAGE

Form and structure [pp. 52–3]

1   'My Last Duchess' uses the dramatic monologue form.

2   'Ozymandias', 'The Prelude', 'My Last Duchess', 'Storm on the Island'

3   Ending every stanza with the word 'sunlight' in 'The Emigrée' foregrounds this word as crucial and makes a lasting impression on the reader, just as it has done on the emigrée herself.

4   'But nothing happens' operates as a refrain in 'Exposure'. This has the effect of creating the same monotony for the reader that the soldiers are experiencing. The use of the 'But' also emphasises that there is an expectation of something happening, as the contrastive connective indicates that this 'nothing' is contrary to normal expectations.

5   The structure of 'War Photographer' shows the outward control that the photographer displays, as the metre is regular and each stanza is end-stopped, echoing the 'ordered rows' of the photographs themselves.

6   Dharker carefully uses repetition of phrases and words to support her themes of construction and creation in 'Tissue'. She repeats the word 'over' when describing the practice of layering and repeats ideas about things 'meant to last' and paper turned 'transparent' to echo this practice in the construction of the poem.

7   'Ozymandias' is a sonnet in that it is fourteen lines using iambic pentameter. The rhyme scheme does not follow either the standard form of Shakespearean or Petrarchan sonnets, but it does have a volta (or turning point), which does not fit into the

rhyme scheme (they usually fall between two clear sections laid out by the rhyme). The imperfect rhyme scheme is usually seen as a critique of Ozymandias's boastful claims.

8   Line 21 of 'The Prelude' is a turning point because this is where the peak begins to appear which changes the boy's view of nature.

9   Agard uses form and structure to indent the 'Caribbean' stanzas and uses italics to separate them. He uses shorter line lengths and no line-initial capitals (except for names). These stanzas therefore appear freer and more lyrical than the 'British' stanzas which use more regular line lengths, rhyme and some initial capitals.

10 • Browning shows how the Duke associates his identity with his 'nine-hundred-years-old name' and presents himself as proud by saying 'I choose never to stoop'. Both of these examples show how Browning uses words and phrases to show the Duke's sense of identity through his class. The poet also uses the poem's construction to show this by using rhyming couplets in iambic pentameter, as this form in drama is traditionally associated with higher-class characters.

   • Agard, however, uses a clash between two different verse forms to represent the difference in Caribbean and British systems that he is presenting in 'Checking Out Me History'. This allows his speaker to show greater affection and respect for the Caribbean figures, through decreased pace which requires the reader to take more time over these stanzas, as well as a mocking use of childish rhyme in some of the 'British' sections.

Rhyme, rhythm and sound [pp. 54–5]

1   'London' uses alternate rhyme.

2   The rhythm in 'The Charge of the Light Brigade' replicates the sound of horses' hoofbeats.

3   Agard's use of dialect supports his theme of identity.

4   Owen's use of part-rhymes in 'Exposure', such as 'knive us' and 'nervous', creates a sense of disharmony and lack of completion or satisfaction. Failing to round off the lines with full rhymes replicates the soldiers' experience of waiting for something that never comes.

5

Device	Quotation	Effect
Onomatopoeia	'thunder'd'	Highlights the cannon fire, while also making it sound like a force of nature against which the soldiers are helpless.
Rhyme	'shell' 'well' and 'Hell'	Foregrounds key words and drives attention to the phrase 'mouth of Hell'.
Alliteration	'shot' and 'shell'	Emphasises the sounds of battle.

6   The rhyme in 'The reader's eyeballs prick / with tears between the bath and pre-lunch beers' links with the theme of attitudes to war as it links the tears with something fun and trivial. This shows that the reader does not take the suffering of those in the photographs very seriously or that they are not affected for very long.

7   Agard seems to use rhyme to mock some of the choices made in the education that the speaker has received. This is particularly evident in the stanza where 'de man who discover de balloon' is rhymed with two nursery rhyme references in 'spoon' and 'moon' before introducing 'Nanny de Maroon'.

8 Owen uses sound including sibilance to contribute to his presentation of nature as hostile. This begins in the first line with 'merciless iced east winds' which uses sibilance to create a hissing effect that evokes malicious intent.

9 The rhymes in 'Ozymandias' continue from the octave (first eight lines) into the sestet (final six lines), gradually introducing new rhymes instead of having two clear sections. Shelley's unique rhyme scheme for a sonnet relates to his themes of corrupt and broken-down power. By not following established rhyming patterns, he creates a disrupted sonnet form which evokes a sense of the decay that he is describing in the poem.

10 • In both 'Exposure' and 'Ozymandias', the poets create a sense of the power of time. While Owen presents time as never-ending and repetitive, through use of the refrain 'But nothing happens', Shelley shows how time has destroyed Ozymandias's great empire: 'Nothing beside remains'.
   • Both poets use rhyme in relatively unusual ways to convey their ideas. For Owen, his over-riding theme is frustration that 'war lasts', shown in the poem's formal elements by part-rhymes which offer no resolution, just as the soldiers are permitted no end to their ordeal. The rhymes are presented in regular ABBAC patterns, but most are part rhymes, such as 'wire'/'war' and 'snow'/'renew', providing a further sense of disharmony.
   • The rhyme in 'Ozymandias', however, is more often straightforward full rhyme, such as 'things'/'kings', but it breaks the pattern of a traditional sonnet. This supports Shelley's themes of corruption and decay, as the poem shows how Ozymandias's power has been lost over time. Shelley creates a new rhyme scheme which does not allow the poem to be broken down into parts as a sonnet traditionally is, but which introduces new rhymes gradually, perhaps echoing the decay of Ozymandias's empire as the 'lone and level sands' gradually replaced it.

Voice and viewpoint [pp. 56–7]

1 'Poppies' is written from the viewpoint of a mother whose son has gone to war.

2 Wordsworth uses the viewpoint of his younger self in 'The Prelude'.

3 The viewpoint used in 'Ozymandias' supports Shelley's message about power because he distances the speaker from Ozymandias by using the 'traveller' who has told the speaker about the statue. This reported speech element makes it more like gossip or hearsay, making Ozymandias himself even less powerful in the present as he is just a story told by a traveller.

4 In 'Kamikaze', the voice shifts show how conflict affects the family through the generations. Moving to the pilot's daughter's voice at the end enables Garland to shift focus from the pilot's decision itself to its impact years later, showing how people stopped speaking in front of him (line 32) and acted as if he had died (line 35). This has much more impact coming from the daughter than it would from the neutral narrator.

5 The third-person viewpoint helps convey the themes in 'Bayonet Charge' by offering an omniscient perspective. Hughes is able to describe what the soldier is feeling and thinking in a moment of confusion, for example comparing him to 'cold clockwork of the stars and nations', which the soldier himself would not be likely to be able to do in that moment.

6 Armitage uses colloquialism and idiom to create the soldier's voice in 'Remains'. The reader is given a clear sense of an ordinary person in an extraordinary situation. Armitage does this with phrases like 'sort of inside out' and 'End of story', which use everyday vocabulary but in context become horrific and shocking.

7 Browning uses imperatives and clear manners to show the Duke's social status and observance of social rules. However, he also uses punctuation, together with caesurae and enjambment, to show how his emotions can get the better of him, for example when explaining his former wife's attitude: 'Somehow – I know not how – as if'.

8 • In both 'Storm on the Island' and 'Exposure', collective viewpoints are important to the themes. Both poems open with first-person plural pronouns which foreground these collective viewpoints: 'Exposure' opens 'Our brains ache', and 'Storm on the Island' opens 'We are prepared'. These both show that the poets are presenting group perspectives and want the reader to see the poems as presenting the experience of a community.
   • Owen's presentation of the soldiers as one is constant throughout 'Exposure' and we do not gain a sense of any individuals separated off from the others. It is central to his presentation of trench experience that this is a shared experience: 'we only know war lasts, rain soaks, and clouds sag stormy'. This tripartite list represents the sum total of the soldiers' knowledge.
   • Similarly, in 'Storm on the Island', Heaney presents the community as united against the storm throughout the poem. There is no sense of an individual experiencing any of the wind's problems, except the second-person 'you' who is occasionally addressed through the poem. In both cases, the collective viewpoint supports the themes by encouraging the reader to see the weather conditions as experienced by a group rather than one individual.

Imagery [pp. 58–9]

1 'Checking Out Me History', 'The Emigrée', 'Tissue'

2 Agard implies the speaker's education has visually impaired him through the imagery of 'Bandage' and 'Blind'.

3 Heaney uses verbs to create increasing violence in 'Storm on the Island'. The wind initially 'pummels your house', which connotes punching repeatedly, then it 'dives and strafes', which are from a military semantic field, and finally it 'bombard[s]'. This increasing violence is created through the connotations of these verbs.

4 The 'kites' simile in line 24 of 'Tissue' implies that money and/or the desire for material goods controls people's lives, by suggesting that receipts might 'fly' their lives and therefore be in power over them.

5

Poem	Example	Technique	Effect
'Poppies'	Lines 27, 28	Metaphor	Shows the physical impact of the mother's nerves.
'Bayonet Charge'	'cold clockwork of the stars'	Alliteration and metaphor	Demonstrates how the soldier feels controlled by external forces.
'The Prelude'	'heaving through the water like a swan'	Simile	Implies gracefulness on the part of the boy rowing.

6 **Possible answer:** This shows how the films have come to represent human suffering in the photographer's mind.

ANSWERS

Poetic devices [pp. 60–1]

1 Extract from, 'The Prelude'

2 'An architect could use all this' is an example of ambiguity as 'this' could refer to various things.

3 The semantic field of war is used in the first half of the second stanza of 'The Emigrée': 'tanks', 'frontiers'. This has the effect of reinforcing the idea that her country/city was at war and that was why her family left; it also implies that she is conflicted about being away from home.

4 Irony is used at the end of 'War Photographer' to show the photographer's desensitisation through the adverb 'impassively', despite his earlier frustration at others' lack of reaction to his work.

5 Heaney use personification in various ways in 'Storm on the Island'. He shows how trees and the sea 'might prove company', but immediately argues against this by presenting trees as potentially dangerous and the sea as treacherous in the simile 'like a tame cat turned savage'.

6

Poem	Quotation(s)	Technique	Effect
'Charge of the Light Brigade'	'Was there a man dismay'd?'	Rhetorical question	Reminds readers of the soldiers' bravery.
'Exposure'	'Pale flakes with fingering stealth come feeling for our faces'	Personification	Presents the snow as maliciously attacking the soldiers.
'My Last Duchess'	'Even had you skill / In speech – (which I have not)'	Irony	Shows the Duke's false modesty and knowledge of social norms – pretending to be modest was appropriate.
'Tissue'	'The light' (1), 'luminous' (26), 'daylight' (29)	Semantic field	Links ideas together and presents tissue/paper as beautiful and having purity as well as being fragile/vulnerable.

7 **Possible answer:** The positioning of this sentence after Ozymandias's boast is ironic because it underlines how everything has been lost over time and the juxtaposition of this statement to the inscription makes it ridiculous.

Tone and mood [p. 62]

1 The tone of 'Exposure' is depressing.

2 The mood of 'The Prelude' shifts with the phrase 'a huge peak, black and huge' as the speaker's fear becomes clear in that moment with the repetition of 'huge' and the switch to simplistic vocabulary, which implies he is unable to think clearly through his fear.

3 The final line of 'Remains', 'His bloody life in my bloody hands', leaves the reader with a complex mood. We see the speaker at once stained with guilt and frustrated by those feelings, almost believing he shouldn't have them, expressed through the mild expletive of 'bloody' which here serves a double purpose.

4 The complex verb forms in the final stanza of 'Kamikaze' contribute to the poem's tone by highlighting the detachment of the narrator. The reader is reminded that this is reported speech, and that no-one knows the pilot's feelings for certain as no-one has spoken to him for years, so the tense form expresses supposition (line 41).

5 **Possible answer:** This has the effect of taking the poem into the realm of the imaginary by using the conditional 'if' to signal that shift. The reader recognises that the poem is about to progress into flights of fancy, which it does by discussing buildings which 'fall away on a sigh'.

PART FIVE: COMPARING POEMS

Evaluating poems [p. 64]

1 Reading activity: no answer required.

2 Memory

3 **Possible answer:** The mother's memories in 'Poppies', moreover, seem to bring her comfort and intrude while she sees her son off to war. The war photographer's memories, however, cause his hands to 'tremble' now that he is safely away from danger. Weir, therefore, presents memories as operating to link events together for the mother and to perhaps offer her solace when her son is away, implying that she will always be able to recall happy memories, such as the one described in lines 12–13. For Duffy's war photographer, however, who has personal experience of wars, memories are more dangerous and the contrasts between home and work can produce terrifying images of 'fields which … explode beneath the feet / of running children in a nightmare heat'.

Using connectives [p. 65]

1 In 'London', Blake's exploration of power is rooted in his eighteenth-century context. This is clear in the industrial vocabulary such as the 'chimney-sweeper' and the reference to the French Revolution with the threat of 'blood' running 'down palace walls'. On the other hand, as a more modern poet, Agard, writes much more directly against the system of government and education with the dismissive pronoun 'dem'.

As a result, Blake's work has a more contemplative mood, while Agard's poem has a fury to it borne of awareness of injustice. This is perhaps also linked to the poems' viewpoints as Blake writes from the third person, but Agard's first-person perspective lends itself to a more indignant expression.

2 On the other hand; both; and; while

Using quotations [p. 66]

1 'But nothing happens' (2); 'Cannon to right of them, / Cannon to left of them' (1); 'six hundred' (4); 'nothing' (3)

2 **Pair 1:** 'Bandage up me eye' and 'mind-forged manacles' – comparison point about oppression (or use of metaphor)
Pair 2: 'he sought approval / without words to do what someone must' and 'myself and somebody else and somebody else' – comparison point about responsibility

Writing a comparison [p. 67]

1 Compare how poets present ideas about the power of nature in 'Storm on the Island' and 'The Prelude'.

2 **Possible answer:** Both 'Storm on the Island' and 'The Prelude' feature the power of nature as a key theme. For example, in 'Storm on the Island', Heaney shows how the sea is untrustworthy through the simile 'like a tame cat turned savage', which shows its unpredictability and violence. In the same way,

Wordsworth reveals the awesome power of nature in 'The Prelude' through a simile using personification when the peak 'like a living thing / strode after me', demonstrating the unexpected malice the speaker experienced through the power of nature. So both poets use imagery to show how nature can be seen as unexpectedly or suddenly violent.

PART SIX PROGRESS BOOSTER

Key skills and using quotations [pp. 69–70]

2 **Student A:** Level: Mid
   Why? Mid-level because there is some detail in the explanation but it lacks detail about Agard's methods in writing the poem.
   Student B: Level – High
   Why? High-level because this links the explanation of the effect to Agard's use of poetic techniques.

3 b)

4 Because 'won't flush him out' implies that the speaker has been trying to remove memories of the experience from his mind, whereas the other two options are focused on the experience in the moment itself.

5 When the war photographer is back home, the speaker describes England as having 'ordinary pain which simple weather can dispel', which shows how his attitude to home has changed because of his experiences observing war. This reveals a critical attitude towards people at home because he now appears dismissive of pain that will just go away because of a change in the weather, which he now sees as 'simple'.

6 When Rumens writes 'I am branded by an impression of sunlight', it conveys the idea that the emigrée is permanently scarred by the idea of where she comes from, even though she simultaneously presents the positive idea of 'sunlight'. She uses the metaphor 'branded' to imply that it has been burned into her. However, in 'My Last Duchess', Browning presents the character of a Duke who takes extreme pride in his family background having 'a nine-hundred-years-old name', but with no accompanying sense of violence to himself. It is immediately clear that his sense of self and relationship with his background is far less complex than that shown in 'The Emigrée'.

Using structure and paragraphs effectively [pp. 71–2]

1 **Topic sentence:** Hughes presents inner conflict as the soldier faces a crisis when crossing the battlefield.

   Quotation: 'clockwork' from 'In what cold clockwork of the stars and the nations'
   Explanation: ... shows the lack of control the soldier feels over his destiny.

2 **Possible answer:** Duffy presents the photographer's attitude to war as respectful, particularly towards those affected by the wars. This is clear where she compares him to 'a priest preparing to intone a Mass'. Using the noun 'priest' suggests a reverential attitude, and saying that he is 'preparing' implies that he is taking his work seriously.

3 **Topic sentence:** Weir presents the mother and son in Poppies as strongly connected through their many shared memories…
   Example: Line 4
   Link to another part of the poem: Later, she resists her desire to show similar tenderness (line 14), as she realises that he has grown up too much for such gestures.
   Linking words or phrases: evokes; Later; as

4 **Possible answer:** Tennyson gives us a vivid picture of the soldiers in order to show their bravery. This is shown through the clear

message that they do not give up even though not many of them are going to survive the battle. When they go into 'the valley of Death', this is pointed out to show that they know they will die, but they go into it anyway, suggesting that they show an attitude of bravery. This is further highlighted through 'sabring the gunners', which emphasises that they are fighting with only swords against guns but they keep fighting. The poem appears to be written to celebrate them because of the bravery they display.

Making inferences and interpretations [p. 73]

1 **Topic sentence:** The speaker's understanding of nature is shown to change in the poem.
   Development of point: We see this in the shift in tone of his descriptions, which starts with pretty imagery such as 'small circles glittering idly'.
   Inference/wider interpretations: This is beautiful but reveals his sense of purposelessness in nature's beauty at this point.

2 b), because the verb 'tosses' implies a casual attitude to the man's body.

Writing about context [p. 74]

1 … the violence that was beginning at that time to spring up between groups with different political and religious beliefs in Northern Ireland.

2 b), because the semantic field represents the gradual increase in ammunition and military-style violence, which mirrors real-world events in Ireland at the time.

3 **Possible answer:** Owen's personal experience as a soldier obviously colours his poetry and, in fact, 'Exposure', along with many other poems, was written in the trenches late in the First World War. This may explain the darker tone that this poem has when compared to some earlier war poetry, which may have a more glorifying tone. Owen's direct experience allows for more poignant description, such as 'we cringe in holes' which is likely to have a strong impact on the reader. The verb 'cringe' here creates a strong impression of soldiers hiding in the trenches, while using 'holes' instead of 'trenches' almost likens the soldiers to animals.

Tackling exam tasks [pp. 75–6]

1 Compare how writers present ideas about inner conflict in 'The Prelude' and one other poem from the cluster.

Sample answers [pp. 77–82]

1 A

4 **Student A – Level: Mid**
   Why? It is a straightforward explanation that offers a sense of poem as a story rather than a piece of crafted literature with any intent on the writer's part
   Student B – Level: High
   Why? It offers more depth of analysis, links within the poem and a clearer awareness of the poem as a crafted piece of writing (reference to Wordsworth as a writer).

6 **Summing up sentence:** Both poems, then, explore and seem to recommend particular attitudes to conflict or to those who have participated in conflict.
   Point suggesting differences: … while 'The Charge of the Light Brigade', written at a very different time
   Final recap sentence: Ultimately, differences in context – Duffy speaking to a war photographer friend, Tennyson reading newspaper reports of the battle, as well as different expectations

ANSWERS

of Victorian and twentieth-century audiences – are a key reason for differences in attitude within the poems.

Final quotation: 'honour' from 'The Charge of the Light Brigade'

8 a) Rewrite sentences more succinctly.

b) 'Zoom in' on quotations to describe effect.

c) Try to compare how the poets write about the theme, not just what they say about it (even if they do it completely differently, e.g. one uses this technique, one that).

10 a) Refers to more than one part of 'Bayonet Charge'.

b) It is better written, with clearer and more effective use of sentences.

c) It begins to 'zoom in' and think about the impact of individual words.

13 The sample response provided is a High-level response because it:

• compares poems in a detailed and well-structured way, moving fluently between ideas in the two poems

• offers convincing ideas and different interpretations and perspectives on the poems

• analyses and explores the poets' methods and effects with insight, and a sound knowledge of poetic terminology

• includes well-chosen quotations and references and embeds them fluently in sentences.